SUPERNORMAL

ANDREW MCCONNELL
28 SUPPLIERS, 89 RECIPES, 26 COOKS

FOR JO

IN LOVING MEMORY OF OUR
DEAR FRIEND PAUL LEE –
YOU ARE GREATLY MISSED.

EARL CARTER, PHOTOGRAPHY
STUDIO ROUND, DESIGN CONCEPT
MICHAEL HARDEN, EDITOR

Hardie Grant
BOOKS

CONTENTS

CONTENTS (CONTINUED)

CONTENTS (CONTINUED)

There's no straightforward origin story about Supernormal. The tale certainly embraces Asia — Japan and China in particular — but it's equally about something personal that's evolved over many years. It's about Melbourne and Hong Kong, Shanghai and Tokyo. It's an amalgamation of source and inspiration, traditional and new, memory and experience, all fitting together in a way that, to me at least, seems perfectly logical (01). And delicious. I suppose the story of Supernormal is really the story of the way I like to eat.

I've been interested in Asian food for as long as I can remember and have cooked it at home for many years. However, professionally my training and experience was all about classical European cooking. Then in 1995 I went to live and work in China, to head kitchens in Hong Kong and Shanghai, cooking European food in upmarket settings but without all the fine dining pomp and ceremony.

I stayed for five years, eating Chinese food twice a day and having a team of 20 to 30 Chinese chefs working with me, three of whom were employed just to cook staff meals. Two of these were older ladies who would cook six to ten of the most incredibly delicious dishes every night. I also went to people's homes and experienced the wonder and variety of Chinese home cooking — and there was always the welcome presence of the incredibly vibrant street food culture (02).

While never taking this food for granted, the constant exposure over five years normalised it in some ways. It became intrinsic to the way I ate and, I realised after returning to Melbourne with no easy access to those same flavours, it was the way I wanted to keep eating. But while part of being back became about missing some of my favourite flavours, the different environment also allowed me to see ways of interpreting the way I cooked this kind of food.

01
Kappabashi Street, Tokyo (Kitchen Town).

02
'There is cause for celebration because the fishermen have caught very good quality tuna.'

9

When cooking Chinese food, I always try to keep in mind that, while it might be my take on a dish, the final product has to remain respectful of the source. Start trying to completely reinvent the wheel and you can quickly lose sight of what was good about the dish in the first place and end up with some kind of scary fusion car crash.

Back in Australia, I consciously began to change the way I cooked Asian food. I was very conscious of using the best produce, cooking it carefully; using corn starches and fats sparingly not excessively, lightening the recipes without losing their flavour profile — in other words, applying some of the principles and techniques that I was using in my restaurants to the Asian cooking I was doing at home.

03
One of the rare remaining cars co-built by Yamaha and Toyota, a 1967 Toyota 2000GT, designed by Satoru Nozaki.

This approach was very much influenced by Japan (03). I first went to Japan while I was based in China and have been back many times since. Japanese food is what I like to eat and, increasingly, Japanese-style has become the way I like to cook too. Japanese flavours are a lot more direct than many cuisines and have a confidence in simplicity. And, while some base ingredients in Japanese cooking have certainly influenced me strongly and have a permanent place in my pantry, it's actually the Japanese approach to cooking that has influenced me more than any particular ingredient or recipe.

04
Favourite mandoline from Tokyu Toyoko Department Store, Shibuya.

I have often found that restaurant cooking in Japan relies on a central core ingredient with only a few layers added to that. It brings a purity and more direct flavour profile to the food compared, say, to Shanghai cooking, where there might be vinegars, sugars, soys, starches and aromatics to make up a dish (04). Japanese cooking might be as simple as a piece of meat, some water, some dried mushrooms, a dash of sauce and some kombu. It shows balance and restraint when something as simple as a piece of tofu with some sesame can stand alone when it's executed well. My experience of the Japanese approach to cooking has given me the confidence and awareness to know when to stop adding to a dish. How to make it about essence rather than excess.

It took ten years after leaving China before I was ready to cook Asian-inspired food in a restaurant. Golden Fields opened in St Kilda in 2011 and in some ways was a prototype for Supernormal with its mix of Chinese, Korean and Japanese dishes with an Australian interpretation. But there were some parameters.

Ultimately, as I tried to work out what I wanted, it became clear I needed to find a balance that referenced my experiences but interpreted them to reflect how I loved to cook and eat (05). What I wanted to do, it turns out, was Supernormal.

We had secured a site for the new restaurant at the street level of a brand new building in Flinders Lane in Melbourne's CBD, a skyscraper that was being built to a six-star energy efficiency rating. The inevitable building delays were compounded by the pioneering nature of the energy efficient construction and, with Golden Fields morphing into a modern French bistro called Luxembourg, we found ourselves with a committed team ready for action and about five months before we would be anywhere near opening.

Not wanting to lose the staff, we decided to do a pop-up called Supernormal Canteen. I had access to an empty space on Gertrude Street in Fitzroy, next to my restaurant Cutler & Co. Dion Hall from Projects of Imagination, who'd done the plans for Supernormal in the city, did the Canteen fitout using some of the signature elements — the graphics, some red neon, the blend of concrete and timber, the general Japanese aesthetic — and applying them to this smaller, two-room space. We originally planned on opening for a month. It stayed open the entire summer.

The Canteen proved integral in defining what Supernormal would be (06). It became an opportunity to keep going with the evolution of the project. We started calling it the Supernormal Test Kitchen, not just because it allowed us to test drive and refine dishes and to change the way we structured and focused the menu, but also because it allowed us a freedom to experiment with the whole concept. It changed things so that Supernormal became both looser and more focused.

05
'The claw' — Dion Hall's coat rack
(bronze cast from chicken feet)
from Golden Fields.

06
Supernormal Canteen.

Japanese flavour and technique came more prominently into the mix at the Canteen. There were lots of cold and raw dishes that changed the way we cooked. We started using dashi in our vinaigrettes and sauces, and made a point of not doing any dish we'd done previously, aside, of course, from the lobster roll that I'll probably be making until the day I stop working in restaurants (perhaps not even then). We shortened the wine list and made music more of a focus, though we left the karaoke until we had a dedicated room (with soundproofing), downstairs in the city restaurant (07).

07
Doorway, concrete and timber.
Omotesando, Tokyo.

Working with the limited resources and temporary nature of the pop-up showed us how to simplify and deformalise. I'd always wanted Supernormal to feel like a canteen, somewhere that had the colour, the mood and the pace of a European train station — it's why we have the long bar, so that solo diners feel comfortable in here too — but with a level of service and comfort that would refine the canteen idea (08).

08
Tokyu Toyoko Department
Store food hall, Shibuya.

I certainly wanted it to have a buzz, which is why there was always going to be an open kitchen. I like the energy of open kitchens. They bring a room to life through sights and smells, by way of the produce being cooked in plain sight and the chefs at work; sensory experiences that you just can't add to a closed dining room.

It's also why we structured the menu the way we did. Supernormal needed a sort of canteen/diner feel, with small dishes you'd come back for if you only had a short time to eat, but with enough on the menu for you to make a night of it if you wanted. It's why we have cheap, quick lunch specials like tonkatsu sandwiches and ramen, so city workers can get a quick fix (09). It's why we serve things in half sizes so people can try more flavours.

09
Japanese fast food.

The menu is shorter than originally planned, because a more compact menu where you can nail all the dishes is a better proposition than one that takes a 'something for everybody' approach and everything ends up just OK.

No straight path led from Point A (idea) to Point B (opening the doors of your new restaurant) at Supernormal. Error and delay were as integral to its final form as planning and concept. The food is based in Asia but it is also about something very personal that's evolved over time. It's been inspired by any number of sources. And when you put those all together, it's Supernormal (10).

Andrew McConnell

10
Untitled.

(Andrew McConnell) My brief to Dion was to create something that felt like a canteen, that wasn't too slow, something with track marks and history, a place you can use and a place you can come back to. It was a long process — the dialogue went on over a year. We were lucky to have so long. We explored in Melbourne but we also travelled to Japan to look at how things were built and what materials worked well together.

(Dion Hall) Travelling through Japan was the nucleus of the creative journey. For me, Tokyo is a wonderful chaotic sensory explosion, harmonised by some magical states of balance. The tension between 'the natural' and 'the mechanical' is drawn into quiet moments throughout Supernormal, where the materials we used capture these personal experiences and all have a story to tell (01).

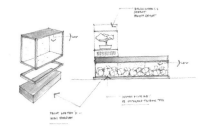

01
Sketch for plant cabinet.

Supernormal is embedded with certain Japanese formulas — simple and limited materials, miniature moments, a series of quiet stories, symbolism. One of the principal drivers of this project was wabi sabi, the aesthetic philosophy rooted in Zen Buddhism, which embraces and accepts imperfection. This applied not just to the use of materials but also to the idea of allowing the design of Supernormal to evolve through compromise and substitution. It was a challenging way to work because Melbourne design has a largely European vernacular where imperfection is something you wrestle with and we were trying to approach it in a more abstract, Japanese way.

(AMc) It was important to me that the place had a certain feel, a particular buzz but with enough space so that it would breathe and flow and be acoustically comfortable. It needed to have a certain sculptural element to it (02).

02
Sketch for praying mantis wall.

(DH) One of the fascinating notions when designing is that it isn't the things you see that matter the most but the things you feel. The great design moment we seek is when a material, an object, or the whole space itself transcends its primary expression and becomes illuminated with meaning. The idea of the whole being more than a sum of its parts (03). Supernormal reflects the belief that a space is inherently more valuable by what it is made from rather than what it is made of. It's the thing you feel rather than see.

03
Initial sketch design for Supernormal
© Projects of Imagination (see overleaf).

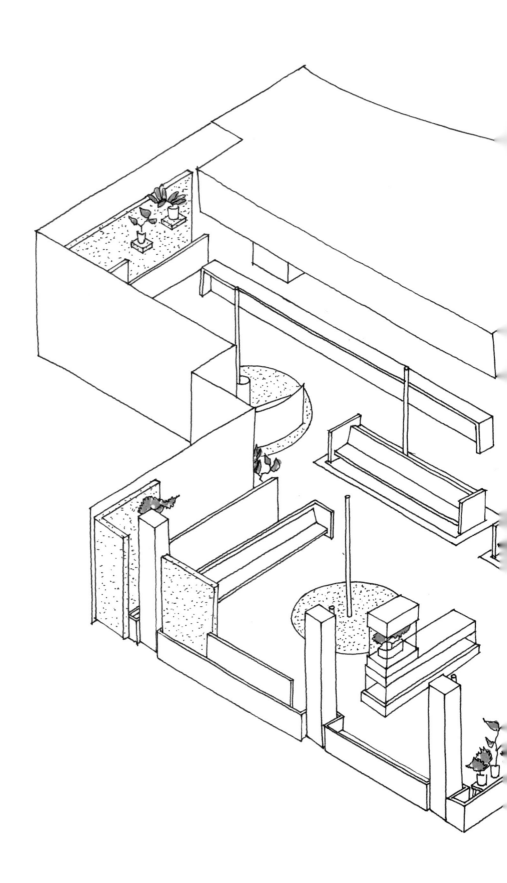

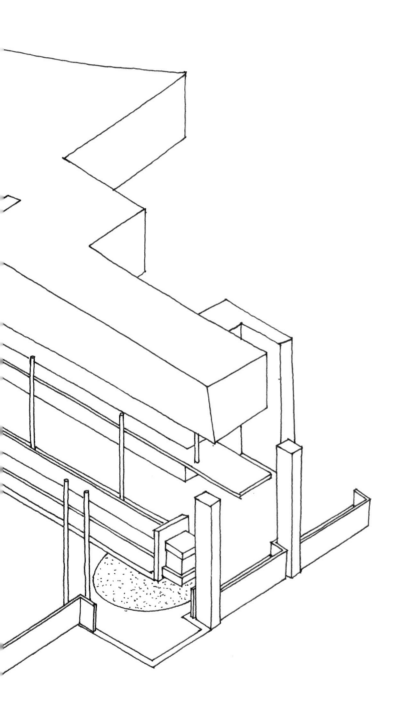

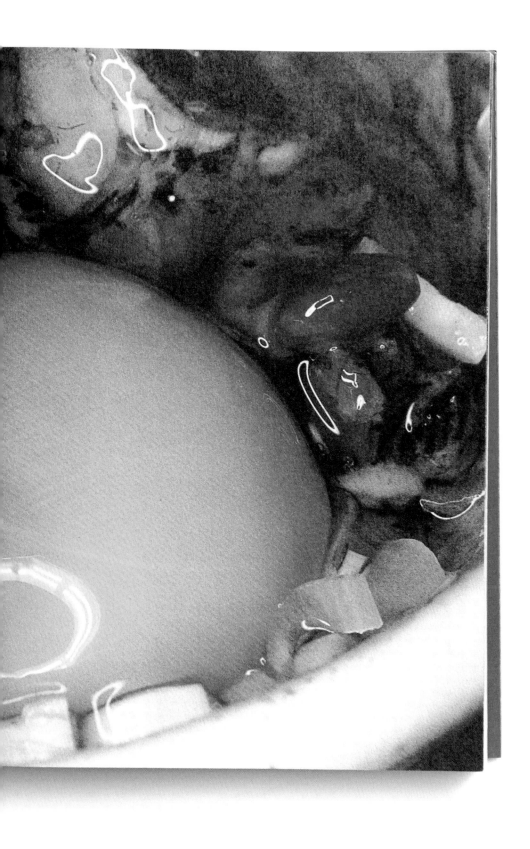

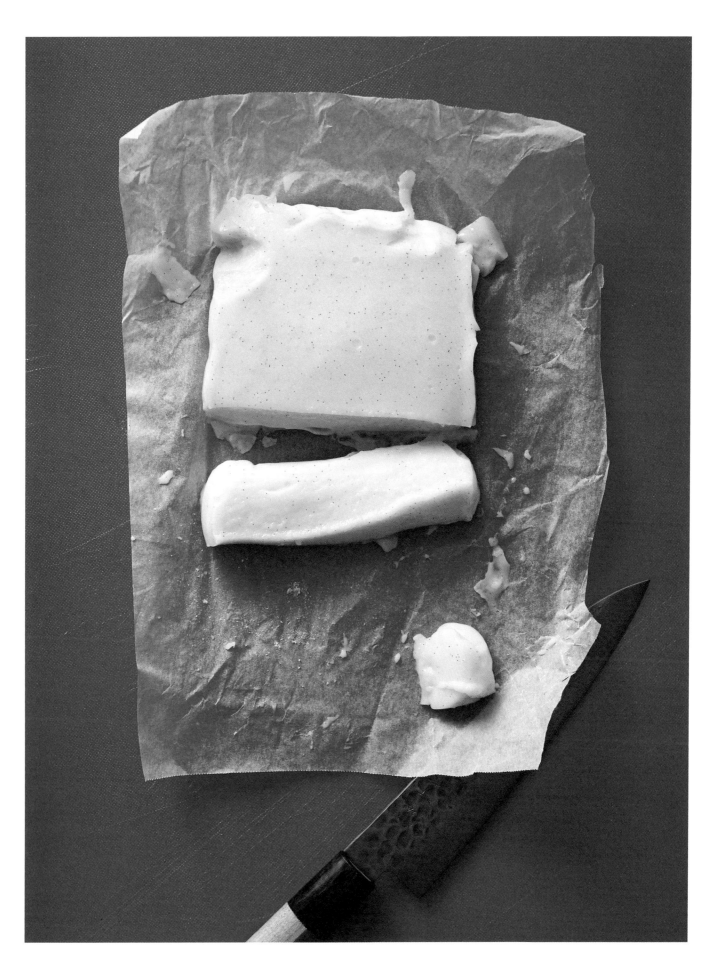

もも
あかつき
中 200えん

完熟

These small but big-flavoured dishes were conceived with the bar in mind, but they work equally well as side dishes or as part of a larger banquet — or, even better, as something you can raid the refrigerator for at midnight. They're a nod to those who, like me, enjoy a mid afternoon pitstop of a quick beer and a little something to eat. They're also ideal for the kind of transient meal that's popular in Melbourne's CBD these days, where people move from one place to the next, having a drink and a snack in a number of different venues. We get a lot of people at the bar at Supernormal who eat this way. It's social and casual and pretty loose in some ways, but it still has its own structure, kind of like bar snacks themselves.

Doing it properly requires awareness — when it comes to balance there's as much science as there is art to bar snacks. To get this balance right I tend to steer away from the more conventional Western type of bar snack and include a mix of things that are raw or crisp or crunchy or cold — the sort of flavours and textures that you might find in an izakaya in Japan or in bars in Hong Kong and Shanghai. Salt is always good in bar snacks but so are fermented foods and vinegar.

The great thing about these sorts of snacks is that they're versatile. They can take the edge off your hunger, stimulate your appetite before a larger meal or simply make a knock-off drink more pleasurable. They can also morph into the main meal, acting as a side dish or accompaniment. In fact, they're good company, bar-side or not.

CANDIED WALNUTS WITH TOASTED NORI

This recipe is based on a snack I first ate in Hong Kong.
It has an arresting flavour that's both sweet and savoury.

Preheat the oven to 170°C (340°F) and line a baking tray with baking paper.

Bring a medium saucepan of water to the boil. Add the walnuts
and bring the water back to the boil. Immediately drain the walnuts
and set aside.

In a small saucepan over medium heat, warm the glucose and sugar.
Add the walnuts and stir quickly to coat them thoroughly. As you stir
the walnuts, gradually sprinkle in the sesame seeds so they evenly
coat the nuts.

Spread the walnuts on the lined baking tray and bake in the oven
for 15–20 minutes, stirring every 5 minutes until the nuts are toasted.

Meanwhile, toast the nori in the oven for 2 minutes. Fold the toasted
nori in half and shred it finely.

Once the walnuts are baked, sprinkle them with the shredded nori
and season with salt and freshly ground black pepper. Store in an
airtight container after cooling.

MAKES 1 CUP

125 g (4½ oz/1 cup) walnuts
2 tablespoons liquid glucose
1 tablespoon sugar
2 tablespoons sesame seeds
1 sheet nori

←
Order and ordering — keeping the kitchen on track.

We serve these addictive snacks to every table at Supernormal.
Salty from the soy, and with a touch of sugar, they're the perfect way
to start a meal.

Preheat the oven to 170°C (340°F) and line a baking tray with baking paper.

In a bowl, whisk the soy sauce, salt and sugar together with 1 teaspoon
water until the salt and sugar have dissolved. Add the pumpkin seeds and
stir them through the soy mixture until the seeds are thoroughly coated.

Spread the seasoned pumpkin seeds in a single layer on the lined
baking tray. Bake for 15–20 minutes, stirring every 5 minutes until dry,
toasted and lightly caramelised. Store in an airtight container for
2–3 days.

MAKES 2 CUPS (300 G/10½ OZ)
1 tablespoon light soy sauce
½ teaspoon salt
1 teaspoon caster (superfine) sugar
250 g (9 oz/1¾ cups) shelled pumpkin
    seeds (pepitas)

↑
A purchase from Cibi, one of our favourite
places in Melbourne.

This is great as an appetiser, but it's also perfect to temper dishes like the Grilled octopus with fermented chilli (p.101).

In a small saucepan over medium heat, combine the vinegar, the 3 tablespoons sugar, the mirin and soy sauce and cook until the sugar has dissolved, taking care not to let it boil. Remove the pan from the heat and set aside to cool.

Soak the wakame in 250 ml (8½ fl oz/1 cup) water for 10 minutes until it is rehydrated.

Slice the cucumbers lengthways into strips and toss them with the salt and the ½ teaspoon sugar. Transfer them to a colander set over a bowl and leave for 10 minutes to drain. Reserve the pickling liquid.

Strain the wakame and squeeze out any excess water.

Pat the cucumbers dry and combine them with the wakame. Add the pickling liquid and leave to macerate for at least 2 hours before serving.

SERVES 4 (AS AN APPETISER)
125 ml (4 fl oz/½ cup) rice wine vinegar
3 tablespoons caster (superfine) sugar, plus ½ teaspoon extra
2 tablespoons mirin
2 tablespoons light soy sauce
10 g (¼ oz) dried wakame
150 g (5½ oz) baby cucumbers (about 6)
½ teaspoon salt

SESAME CUCUMBERS

In 2013 my development chef, John Paul Twomey, and I were invited to cook on Shodoshima Island in Japan as part of the Setouchi International Art Festival. On the opening day of the event a large yakitori welcome dinner was served by the locals. The banquet we were served included these lightly cured and seasoned cucumbers rolled in toasted sesame seeds — crunchy, sweet and savoury.

Mix together the vinegars and soy sauce in a bowl and set aside.

Peel 3 strips of skin off the cucumbers, lengthways, creating a striped pattern running the length of each cucumber. Submerge the cucumbers in the vinegar mixture and refrigerate overnight.

Grind the sesame seeds using a mortar and pestle until you have a coarse meal.

Remove the cucumbers from the pickling liquid and impale each one lengthways on a bamboo skewer.

Spread the ground sesame seeds on a plate. Roll the cucumbers through the ground seeds to evenly coat them. Serve immediately.

SERVES 6

80 ml (2½ fl oz/⅓ cup) sweet
  ginger vinegar
60 ml (2 fl oz/¼ cup) rice wine vinegar
2 tablespoons soy sauce
6 baby cucumbers
3 tablespoons sesame seeds, toasted
6 short bamboo skewers

In China, variations of marinated cucumber are often served at the start of a meal. I don't usually enjoy marinated food straight from the refrigerator, but this is an exception with the chill of the refrigerator enhancing the crunch of the cucumber.

To make the dressing, soak the garlic and ginger together in water for 5 minutes. Strain and place in fresh water for another 5 minutes. Repeat this process twice more then strain and dry on paper towel. When dry, mix with the soy sauce, sesame oil and sugar. If chilli is your thing, add a good splash of chilli oil to the dressing.

Halve the radishes if they are small or quarter them if they are large.

Put the radishes and cucumbers in a bowl and mix through the salt and sugar. Transfer to a colander set over a bowl to drain in the refrigerator for 30 minutes. Pat the vegetables dry and toss them in the dressing.

Place in the refrigerator for an hour before serving.

SERVES 4

1 bunch French breakfast
   or red radishes
6 baby cucumbers, sliced into
   1 cm (½ in) discs
½ teaspoon salt
½ teaspoon sugar

DRESSING

5 garlic cloves, finely chopped
2 teaspoons finely chopped
   fresh ginger
2½ tablespoons light soy sauce
2 tablespoons sesame oil
1 teaspoon sugar
Chinese chilli oil (optional)

↑
Back of house.

↑
Untitled.

This is one of my favourite vegetables and vegetable preparations. I like to serve this at home when we are eating dumplings. It's an especially good snack served with a cold beer.

Toss the kohlrabi and salt together in a bowl.

Transfer the kohlrabi to a colander set over a bowl and leave to drain for 30 minutes.

Rinse the kohlrabi in plenty of cold water and drain well.

In a large bowl, combine the salted kohlrabi, kimchi base and garlic chives. Wearing disposable kitchen gloves, mix the kimchi thoroughly through the kohlrabi. Leave the kohlrabi for 3 hours in the refrigerator to marinate before eating. This will keep for up to 4 days.

SERVES 8

3 kohlrabi, peeled and cut
   into 1 cm (½ in) thick batons
1 tablespoon sea salt
200 g (7 oz) Kimchi base (p.219)
75 g (2¾ oz) garlic chives,
   cut into 5 cm (2 in) lengths

FRIED RICE CAKES WITH
KOREAN SWEET CHILLI SAUCE

We've tested many types of Korean rice cakes at Supernormal. The Chongga brand is the best we've found to date. They have great texture, crisp up nicely in the pan and don't seem to soak up much oil at all.

To make the Korean sweet chilli sauce, combine all the ingredients with 60 ml (2 fl oz/¼ cup) water in a saucepan. Bring to the boil then reduce the heat to a simmer. Cook gently for 5 minutes or until the liquid has reduced by half and slightly thickened. Remove the pan from the heat and leave to cool for 30 minutes.

Bring a large saucepan of water to the boil and drop in the rice cakes. Boil for 3 minutes or until soft. Drain them and pat dry with paper towel.

In a non-stick frying pan over high heat, heat half the grapeseed oil until hot. Carefully add half the blanched rice cakes and reduce the heat to medium. Sauté the rice cakes until crunchy, about 3–4 minutes. Remove the cakes and cook the remaining rice cakes in the same manner.

When all the rice cakes are crunchy, place them in a bowl with the Korean sweet chilli sauce. Toss well with the sauce and serve immediately topped with the ground sesame seeds.

See photograph (p.52).

SERVES 6

500 g (1 lb 2 oz) Korean rice cakes
   (we like Chongga brand)
100 ml (3½ fl oz) grapeseed oil
2 teaspoons sesame seeds,
   toasted and coarsely ground

KOREAN SWEET CHILLI SAUCE

4 garlic cloves, finely grated
60 g (2 oz/¼ cup) gochujang
   (Korean chilli paste)
110 g (4 oz/½ cup) sugar
60 ml (2 fl oz/¼ cup) mirin

←
Paul Lee and Andrew at Supernormal.

↑
Paul Lee in the kitchen with Chef Ben.

↑
Chongga brand Korean rice cakes.
←
Fried rice cakes with
Korean sweet chilli sauce (p.51).

We have the wonderful chef Tony Tan to thank for this delicious recipe. You can make a deluxe version by substituting lamb rack cutlets for the lamb ribs, in which case you can skip the steaming and just grill the marinated meat.

Cut off any excess fat from the lamb ribs.

Combine all the spices with the sugar, except the 13-spice and ½ teaspoon of the sea salt. Grind them to a fine powder in an electric spice grinder or use a mortar and pestle.

Coat the lamb ribs with the spice mix, rubbing it into the meat with your hands. Place the ribs in the refrigerator overnight to marinate.

The following day, place the ribs in a steamer over a saucepan of vigorously boiling water. Steam them for 1½–2 hours until the meat is soft and giving. When cooked, place the ribs in the refrigerator to cool.

When ready to serve, slice the ribs into individual pieces and cook on a hot barbecue with no oil, or fry them with a tablespoon of oil in a non-stick frying pan, until golden and caramelised.

Mix together the 13-spice and the ½ teaspoon sea salt.

Serve the lamb ribs immediately, sprinkled with the spiced salt, and with the lemon cheeks on the side.

SERVES 8

2 kg (4 lb 6 oz) lamb ribs,
   intact as whole plates
2 tablespoons ground,
   roasted dried chillies
1½ teaspoons sea salt
1 tablespoon coriander seeds
1 tablespoon black peppercorns
1 tablespoon Sichuan peppercorns
3 teaspoons white peppercorns
2 star anise
4 cloves
115 g (4 oz/½ cup firmly packed)
   brown sugar
1 tablespoon grapeseed oil (optional)
½ teaspoon ground 13-spice
   or Chinese five-spice
cheeks of 2 lemons

Preheat the oven to 170°C (340°F) and line a baking tray with baking paper.

Mix the peanuts through the grapeseed oil then spread them out in a single layer on the lined baking tray. Roast in the oven for 6–8 minutes, or until golden. Remove the peanuts and leave them to drain and cool on paper towel.

Meanwhile, in a small saucepan over medium–low heat, bring the vinegars, sugar, salt, star anise, peppercorns and five-spice to a simmer. Cook for 5 minutes or until reduced by half. Strain through a fine sieve, discard the solids and set the syrup aside.

In a bowl, combine the peanuts with the vinegar syrup and pickled mustard stem, mixing well to coat the peanuts thoroughly. Season with a pinch of five-spice and sea salt flakes to taste. These are best eaten on the day they are made.

SERVES 4–6 (AS A SNACK)

200 g (7 oz/1¼ cups) raw peanuts

60 ml (2 fl oz/¼ cup) grapeseed oil

60 ml (2 fl oz/¼ cup) balsamic vinegar

60 ml (2 fl oz/¼ cup) Chinese brown rice vinegar

1 tablespoon sugar

½ teaspoon sea salt, plus extra to taste

½ star anise

¼ teaspoon white peppercorns

¼ teaspoon Chinese five-spice, plus an extra pinch to serve

2 tablespoons finely chopped pickled mustard stem

PICKLED SHIITAKE MUSHROOMS

Bring a saucepan of salted water to the boil. Add the mushrooms to the boiling water and cook for 1 minute, using a small sieve or kitchen spoon to hold them under the water. Drain the mushrooms and set aside.

Put the vinegar, sugar, soy sauce, 250 ml (8½ fl oz/1 cup) water and the ginger in a small saucepan over medium heat and cook until the sugar has dissolved, taking care not to let it boil.

Remove the pan from the heat and pour the liquid over the mushrooms. Leave to pickle for at least 2 hours before using. Drain the liquid before serving. These keep nicely in the refrigerator for up to a week.

SERVES 8 (AS A SNACK)

500 g (1 lb 2 oz) fresh shiitake mushrooms, stems removed
125 ml (4 fl oz/½ cup) rice wine vinegar
110 g (4 oz/½ cup) sugar
125 ml (4 fl oz/½ cup) light soy sauce
1 tablespoon thinly sliced fresh ginger

↑
Disproportionately large container for shiitake pickling (a pet hate).

This makes a great snack or canapé. I have from time to time used the crab mixture in this recipe to make a very mean sandwich.

Remove 8 small crisp inner leaves from the lettuce. Wash the leaves, dry them well and place in the refrigerator until ready to serve.

In a bowl, mix together the crabmeat, Kewpie mayonnaise and lemon juice. Season to taste with the salt and ground fennel.

In a saucepan over medium heat, fry the curry leaves in the grapeseed oil until they are crisp and translucent. Alternatively, brush the leaves with a little oil and dry them out in the microwave on High (100%) in 15-second bursts of heat until crisp. When crisp, transfer to paper towel to drain. Sprinkle the leaves with a little salt.

Divide the crab mixture between the lettuce leaves and top each with a few fried curry leaves and a sprinkle of Espelette pepper.

MAKES 8 PIECES

1 head baby cos (romaine)
  or iceberg lettuce
200 g (7 oz) picked, cooked crabmeat
1½ tablespoons Kewpie mayonnaise
1½ teaspoons lemon juice
pinch of sea salt flakes
pinch of ground fennel seeds
handful of fresh curry leaves
1 tablespoon grapeseed oil
pinch of ground Espelette pepper
  or dried chilli flakes

Amaebi prawns can be found at some fishmongers.
If unavailable, small Crystal Bay prawns can be used.

Bring the sugar, soy sauce, Shaoxing rice wine, ginger, shallot and
150 ml (5 fl oz) water to a simmer in a saucepan over medium heat.
Continue to simmer gently for 5 minutes. Transfer to a container
and leave in the refrigerator to cool.

Bring a large saucepan of salted water to a simmer over medium
heat. Plunge the prawns into the water and cook for 30 seconds.
Remove from the heat and cool in plenty of iced water for no more than
a minute. Strain and quickly pat the prawns dry before adding them to
the cool wine marinade. Leave to marinate for 30 minutes before
serving. Serve with a discard bowl for the shells and a finger bowl
for sticky fingers.

SERVES 4

1½ tablespoons sugar
60 ml (2 fl oz/¼ cup) white soy sauce
200 ml (7 fl oz) Shaoxing rice wine
3 cm (1¼ in) piece fresh ginger, sliced
1 French shallot, peeled and
  cut into rings
300 g (10½ oz) amaebi prawns (shrimp)
  or other small prawns

The raw section on the menu at Supernormal is the most purely Japanese part of the list. There are raw dishes in the cuisines of other parts of Asia, but the recipes here are very much about those from Japan — sashimi in particular. Most people — well most of the people who come into Supernormal anyway — seem very comfortable with eating raw fish these days. And it has a lot going for it, especially when the produce is benchmark.

One of the things that I love about Japanese food is the refinement and the hands-off approach in terms of ingredients. Often, the Japanese flavours are a lot more direct and have a purity about them. They often represent the perfect balance between too much and not enough. With raw dishes in particular, there are no layers of flavour to hide behind so it becomes all about the produce.

One of the things that I've really appreciated about working with Japanese food and techniques is the way that it has taught me to have the confidence to leave things alone, to strip things back, to leave just the essential. The essence.

It's also very pleasurable as a chef to have the time to sit and fillet fish. Because of the accuracy and the repetition that's needed for these raw dishes, it becomes almost meditative to carve fish at the same even pace using a perfectly sharp sushi knife. It is well worth your while investing in a good sushi knife — it's one of those tools that not only makes your life easier and the process more pleasurable, but it's beautiful to look at too.

SEAWEED CRACKERS, UNI, PICKLED SHALLOTS

To make the seaweed crackers, in a food processor blend the flour, seaweed paste and salt until combined.

With the machine running, slowly add the water until a dough forms. The dough will feel wet but it should hold together.

On a work surface, lay out two 50 cm (20 in) lengths of plastic wrap, one on top of the other, spreading them out smoothly to make sure there are no bubbles between them.

Shape the cracker dough into a 5 cm (2 in) cylinder and place it along the bottom half of the plastic wrap.

Working quickly, roll the plastic wrap around the dough. Tie off each end, tightening up the cylinder as you do so.

Bring a large saucepan of water, fitted with a steamer, to the boil. Steam the cracker dough over rapidly boiling water for 1 hour, topping up the water if necessary.

Put the cylinder of dough in the refrigerator overnight to firm up.

The next day, remove the plastic wrap and slice the dough cylinder into 1.5 mm (⅛ in) rounds. Place the crackers in a dehydrator on a high setting for 45 minutes, or place the crackers on a baking tray lined with baking paper in a 50°C (120°F) oven for 2–4 hours.

Fill a large, heavy-based saucepan one-third full with grapeseed oil and heat it to 200°C (400°F). Deep-fry one cracker at a time — they only take a couple of seconds to puff up. Scoop them out and transfer to paper towel to drain. If they are chewy, the dough will need to be dried for longer. Once fried, keep the crackers in a sealed container.

When ready to serve, place a piece of uni on each cracker and season lightly with a small pinch of salt. Top with a little pickled shallot and spring onion and serve immediately.

This recipe will make more crackers than you need. Once fried, the crackers will keep indefinitely in the cupboard in an airtight container.

SERVES 8
8 pieces uni (sea urchin)
sea salt
Pickled shallots (p.221)
thinly sliced spring onion (scallion)
    for garnish

SEAWEED CRACKERS
250 g (9 oz) tapioca flour
110 g (4 oz) seaweed paste
2 teaspoons sea salt flakes
125 ml (4 fl oz/½ cup) hot tap
    water (50°C/120°F)
grapeseed oil for deep-frying

BONITO, WASABI LEAF DRESSING, WASABI FLOWERS

A thriving wasabi industry has been established in Tasmania over the past decade or so. The fresh wasabi leaves and flowers have a subtle floral flavour unlike the harsh industrially processed stuff (that often contains no wasabi at all).

In a small saucepan over medium heat, place the vinegar, sugar and salt along with 500 ml (17 fl oz/2 cups) water. Heat until the sugar has dissolved, taking care not to let it boil. Remove the pan from the heat, transfer the liquid to a bowl and allow this pickling liquid to cool in the refrigerator.

If your bonito fillets are small, remove the pin bones with tweezers. If your fillets are larger, remove the bones by using a knife to cut down either side of the central bones and the bloodline.

Submerge the bonito in the pickling liquid and refrigerate for 45 minutes.

To make the wasabi leaf dressing, stir all the ingredients together in a small bowl. Taste and adjust the seasoning with salt if needed.

Remove the bonito fillets from the pickling liquid and pat them dry with paper towel.

Using a blowtorch, scorch the skin side of the fish only until blistered. Alternatively, the fillets can be placed under a hot grill (broiler) or salamander to scorch the skin.

Lay the fillet, skin side up, on a chopping board and slice the bonito into 5 mm (¼ in) slices.

Arrange 5 slices on each serving plate and add 1 teaspoon of dressing on and around the bonito. To finish, arrange the wasabi flower shoots and small leaves on and around the sliced fish.

SERVES 6

250 ml (8½ fl oz/1 cup) rice wine vinegar
140 g (5 oz/⅔ cup) sugar
2 tablespoons salt
400 g (14 oz) bonito fillets, skin on
6 wasabi flower shoots and
    smaller leaves

WASABI LEAF DRESSING

1 tablespoon Spring onion oil (p.219)
1 tablespoon ground wasabi sauce
    (preferably Hawasabi brand)
small pinch of sugar
1 teaspoon lemon juice
1½ teaspoons grapeseed oil
2 wasabi leaves, shredded

←
Bonito, pre- and post-scorching.

COBIA, PICKLED FENNEL,
SOY DASHI DRESSING

Cobia is also known as black kingfish. It has a heavily marbled flesh, which can stand up to the strong flavours of the pickled fennel and yuzu kosho. If cobia is unavailable, kingfish is a good substitute.

To make the soy dashi dressing, mix all the ingredients together in a small bowl.

Cutting horizontally across the fillet, slice the fish into 2 mm (⅛ in) thick long strips.

Lightly spread a pinch of yuzu kosho over each slice of fish.

Place the pickled fennel on a serving plate and arrange the cobia on top. Drizzle with the soy dashi dressing and serve.

SERVES 4 (AS A SMALL STARTER)
200 g (7 oz) cobia fillet, trimmed
1–2 teaspoons yuzu kosho
¼ cup Pickled fennel (p.220)

SOY DASHI DRESSING
3 teaspoons rice wine vinegar
1½ tablespoons shoyu dashi (soy dashi)
3 teaspoons mirin
1½ tablespoons water
1 tablespoon grapeseed oil

Organisation is the key in any kitchen.

TUNA, AVOCADO, WAKAME, PICKLED CUCUMBER

To make the pickled cucumber, in a small saucepan put the vinegar, 125 ml (4½ fl oz/½ cup) water, the sugar and salt and cook until the sugar has dissolved, taking care not to let it boil. Remove from the heat and allow to cool for 10 minutes. Slice the cucumber into 5 mm (¼ in) rounds. Pour the pickling liquid over the cucumber and leave for at least 2 hours.

To make the soy dressing, place all the ingredients in an upright blender except the grapeseed oil and process well. With the blender running, slowly pour the oil in to emulsify the dressing.

Mash the avocado with the milk and push it through a fine sieve.

Process the wakame finely in an electric spice grinder.

To serve, arrange the tuna on a plate and place small spoonfuls of avocado on each piece of fish. Drizzle over 2 teaspoons of the soy dressing. Season the tuna lightly with sea salt. Place one piece of pickled cucumber on each piece of tuna. Place a slice of radish onto each piece of tuna. Sprinkle the whole dish with wakame powder.

SERVES 2-4
¼ avocado
¼ teaspoon milk
½ teaspoon dried wakame
250 g (9 oz) sashimi-grade tuna, trimmed and cut into 1.5 cm (½ in) cubes
¼ teaspoon sea salt flakes
2 small red radishes, thinly sliced

SOY DRESSING
2 tablespoons light soy sauce
½ teaspoon rice wine vinegar
¼ teaspoon caster (superfine) sugar
zest of ¼ lemon
60 ml (2 fl oz/¼ cup) grapeseed oil

PICKLED CUCUMBER
60 ml (2 fl oz/¼ cup) rice wine vinegar
2 tablespoons sugar
2 teaspoons salt
1 baby cucumber, sliced into 5 mm (¼ in) rounds

SEA BREAM, DAIKON, SWEET GINGER DRESSING

Take a mandoline and slice the daikon very thinly. Use a knife to cut the slices into fine julienne. Arrange the daikon on a chilled plate (the daikon can be stored in cold water if you are not using it immediately).

Slice the sea bream fillets on a 45-degree angle into 2 mm (⅛ in) thick slices and lay them over the daikon.

Dress the fish with the sweet ginger dressing, a sprinkling of sea salt flakes and the thinly sliced chives.

Just before serving, wave the sheet of laver over a naked flame to crisp it up (or place it in a preheated 150°C/300°F oven for a moment). Crush the toasted laver in your hands and sprinkle it over the whole dish.

SERVES 4

15 cm (6 in) piece daikon (white radish), peeled
200 g (7 oz) skinless sea bream or porgy fillets
2 tablespoons Sweet ginger dressing (p.219)
½ teaspoon sea salt flakes
1 tablespoon thinly sliced chives
1 sheet sesame laver

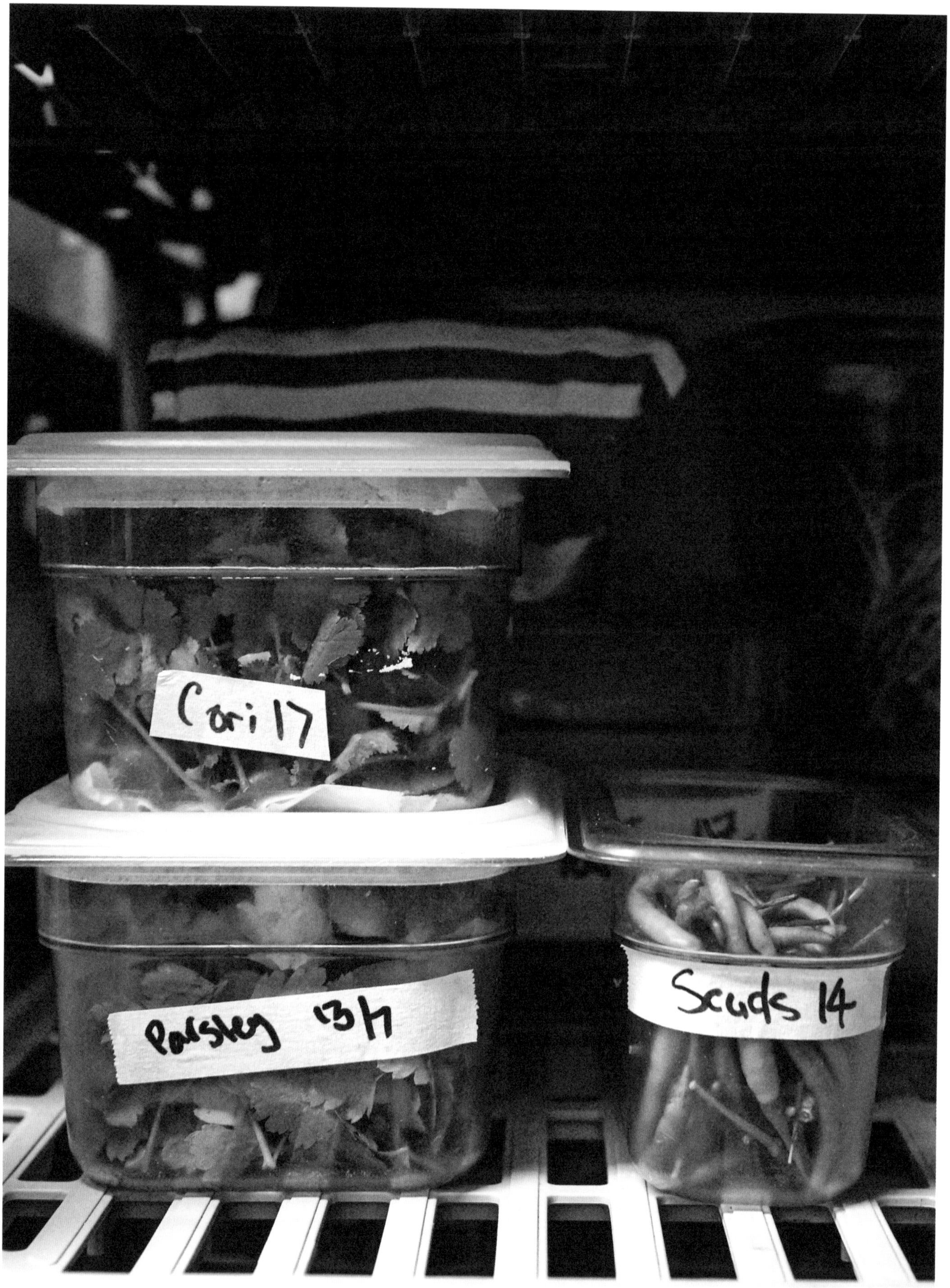
Cori 17
Parsley 13/7
Scuds 14

BEEF TARTARE, CLAM MAYONNAISE, MUSTARD LEAF, SHALLOTS

To make the clam mayonnaise, place a large saucepan over high heat. Add the clams and a splash of water and cover with a lid. Check the clams after 1 minute, stirring them around and replacing the lid. Stir and check each minute until all the clams have opened, then drain them, reserving half the cooking liquid.

Shuck the clams and check that no shell fragments remain. Roughly chop the clam meat and set it aside. You should end up with approximately 80 g (2¾ oz) clam meat. Keep the clams and reserved liquid separate.

In a medium bowl, whisk the egg yolk with the mustard. Slowly pour in half the grapeseed oil, whisking all the time, until emulsified. The mayonnaise will be quite thick at this stage. Mix in the clam meat and 1 teaspoon of the reserved cooking liquid. Slowly whisk in the remaining oil. Season with the salt and lemon juice, adding more reserved liquid if needed. Set the mayonnaise aside.

Remove the mustard green leaves from the stems. Set the stems aside and wash the leaves under cold water.

Preheat the oven to 80°C (175°F) and line a baking tray with baking paper.

Bring a small saucepan of water to the boil and blanch the mustard leaves for 1 minute. Cool the leaves in iced water then drain them and squeeze out any remaining water.

Flatten the leaves and place them on the lined baking tray. Place the leaves in the oven (or in a dehydrator) for 1–2 hours or until crisp.

In a small saucepan over medium heat, gently cook the garlic in the grapeseed oil. Once the garlic has become golden in colour, remove it from the oil with a slotted spoon. Keep the oil and discard the garlic slices. Set the oil aside to cool.

Trim your piece of beef rump and remove all visible sinew. Using a sharp knife, thinly slice the beef and then chop it into very small pieces, like a fine mince.

Place the beef in a small bowl with the garlic oil, preserved mustard stem and a pinch of sea salt, mixing well.

Place 1½ tablespoons of clam mayonnaise on each plate and arrange the beef on top. Grind some black pepper over the beef. Top with pickled shallots, fried shallots and crushed dehydrated mustard leaf.

SERVES 6 (AS A SMALL STARTER)
½ bunch mustard greens
½ garlic clove, thinly sliced
60 ml (2 fl oz/¼ cup) grapeseed oil
400 g (14 oz) beef rump, smoked
2 tablespoons preserved mustard stem, finely chopped
sea salt
2 tablespoons Pickled shallots (p.221)
2 tablespoons Fried shallots (p.221)

CLAM MAYONNAISE
500 g (1 lb 2 oz) surf (large) clams
1 egg yolk
2 teaspoons Dijon mustard
125 ml (4 fl oz/½ cup) grapeseed oil
½ teaspoon salt
1 tablespoon lemon juice

This chapter is a collection of some of my favourite dishes that don't fall easily into any particular category. There are some offal (variety meat) dishes here, and some random things like pork belly and steamed abalone that washed up here too. To me it seems these dishes all belong together, even if they fit together in a way that's not particularly or immediately obvious.

There's certainly a mixed bag of techniques and ingredients. Take some of the offal dishes, for example. One of my favourite things to eat in China is cold cuts. I've used the techniques they use in China to make cold cuts from ingredients like chicken, but here I'm applying them to pig's ear, tongue and brisket elements.

I suppose these small dishes are roughly equivalent to an appetiser in terms of their size but they can be used as stand-alone dishes or as part of a larger shared meal, so they're a lot more versatile than a traditional appetiser. It's the kind of flexibility that you find on menus in Asia and particularly throughout China, where there is a less rigid structure to a meal and I tend to construct a meal according to the way I want to eat at that moment. It's liberating.

SPICY PASTRAMI WITH
CHILLI OIL DRESSING

David Blackmore is one of Australia's best wagyu producers and brisket is one of the best cuts from this animal. Full of flavour with well-marbled fat, it copes brilliantly with the long cooking needed here.

Soak the brisket in water for 24 hours, changing the water 3 times. Drain and pat the meat dry.

To make the pastrami spice mix, preheat the oven to 180°C (350°F).

In a roasting tin, place the coriander, star anise, cloves and all the peppercorns and roast them for 1–2 minutes or until fragrant. Remove the tin from the oven and leave to cool. Use a mortar and pestle or a spice grinder to finely grind the spices. Mix in the rest of the spice mix ingredients. Set aside.

Preheat the oven to 150°C (300°F).

Place the brisket in a deep roasting tin along with the rest of the ingredients. Cover and cook in the oven for 2 hours. Reduce the heat to 110°C (230°F) and cook for a further 4 hours, or until soft and giving when prodded with a chopstick. Check the meat every so often and add more water to the tin if the cooking liquid is evaporating.

To make the chilli oil dressing, whisk all the ingredients together in a small bowl. Set aside.

After 4 hours, remove the brisket from its liquid, pat it dry and coat it liberally with the spice mix. Place the pastrami between two trays and weigh down the top tray with some tins of food or a cast-iron pan. Leave to cool overnight in the refrigerator.

To serve, slice the brisket as thinly as you can and arrange it on a serving plate. Drizzle with a spoonful of chilli dressing.

SERVES 8

1 kg (2 lb 3 oz) corned beef brisket
250 ml (8½ fl oz/1 cup) light soy sauce
1.5 litres (51 fl oz/6 cups) water
½ cup rock sugar
250 ml (8½ fl oz/1 cup) Shaoxing
   rice wine
20 g (¾ oz) fresh ginger, sliced
3 garlic cloves, sliced
1 spring onion (scallion),
   white part only, sliced
1 cinnamon stick
2 star anise
1 teaspoon Sichuan peppercorns

PASTRAMI SPICE MIX
1 tablespoon coriander seeds
2 star anise
3 cloves
2 tablespoons black peppercorns
1 tablespoon white peppercorns
2 tablespoons Sichuan peppercorns
3 tablespoons Korean chilli flakes
1 tablespoon smoked paprika
115 g (4 oz/½ cup firmly packed)
   brown sugar

CHILLI OIL DRESSING
60 ml (2 fl oz/¼ cup) chilli oil
1 teaspoon light soy sauce
1 teaspoon sesame oil
¼ teaspoon Sichuan peppercorns,
   toasted and ground
¼ teaspoon Chinese five-spice

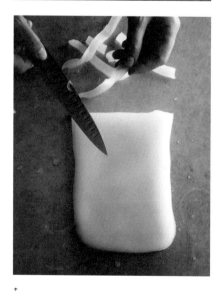

↑
Homemade mung bean noodles.
Work quickly!
Cut noodles to preferred size.

HOMEMADE MUNG BEAN NOODLES,
WHITE CUT CHICKEN, ROASTED SESAME DRESSING

If pressed for time another way to prepare the chicken is to joint it into quarters and steam. Season with plenty of salt before steaming and cool in the refrigerator before using.

To make the roasted sesame dressing, discard the excess oil from the top of the jar of sesame paste. Combine the sesame paste and sugar thoroughly. Slowly whisk in the soy sauce and vinegar. Add the water, 2 teaspoons at a time, until the dressing has the consistency of cream. The sauce will thicken significantly when you start to add the water, but thin out when most of the water has been added. Set the dressing aside.

To make the mung bean noodles, in a small bowl combine the flour and 125 ml (4 fl oz/½ cup) of the cold water, mixing well.

In a medium saucepan over medium heat, bring the remaining cold water to the boil. Whisk the flour slurry into the boiling water and keep whisking until the mixture thickens. Working quickly, pour the mixture into a shallow 20 x 15 cm (8 x 6 in) tray. Tap the tray on a work surface to spread the mixture out and level the surface. Leave to set for 1 hour at room temperature. Once set, turn the noodle sheet carefully out onto a board. Cut the sheet into 3 lengthways, and then make 1 cm (½ in) slices across to produce 5 cm (2 in) long batons. Lightly coat the noodles in the sesame oil and set aside.

To prepare the chicken, begin by rinsing it under cold water. Drain. Remove any excess fat and skin from the cavity and around the neck. Cut off and discard the parson's nose. Remove the legs from the chicken.

Put the chicken and the legs in a large saucepan, wide enough to fit the chicken snugly and deep enough to cover it with water. Add the chopped spring onion pieces to the pan, along with the salt, ginger, peppercorns, half the coriander sprigs and enough water to cover the chicken by 2.5 cm (1 in). Cover the pan with a lid and bring to the boil. Reduce the heat and simmer very gently for 5 minutes. Turn the heat off and leave the chicken in the covered pan for a further 10 minutes.

Place the saucepan in the refrigerator and allow to cool completely.

Once the chicken is cool, remove it from the pan and pat it dry. Shred the meat from the legs and season with a pinch of salt. Remove the breast meat from the crown and carve it into 1 cm (½ in) thick slices.

In a stainless steel bowl, toss the noodles and shredded chicken with the sesame oil. Arrange the noodles across six serving plates. Spoon 1 tablespoon of roasted sesame dressing over each plate of noodles. Top with some cucumber, followed by the sliced chicken. Drizzle each plate with chilli oil and add a pinch of ground Sichuan pepper. Finish the dish with the peanuts, sliced spring onion and the remaining coriander.

SERVES 6 (AS AN APPETISER)
1 x 1.6 kg (3½ lb) whole chicken
1 spring onion (scallion),
    cut into 5 cm (2 in) pieces,
    plus 15 g (½ oz/¼ cup) thinly sliced
    spring onion to serve
1 tablespoon salt
1 slice fresh ginger
½ teaspoon white peppercorns
10 coriander (cilantro) sprigs
1 teaspoon sesame oil
1 Lebanese (short) cucumber,
    peeled and julienned
1 tablespoon chilli oil
1 teaspoon Sichuan pepper,
    toasted and ground
2 tablespoons peanuts,
    roasted and roughly chopped

ROASTED SESAME DRESSING
100 g (3½ oz) jar roasted sesame paste
3 teaspoons caster (superfine) sugar
2 tablespoons soy sauce
2 tablespoons rice wine vinegar
2 tablespoons water, approximately

MUNG BEAN NOODLES
35 g (1¼ oz/¼ cup) mung bean flour
625 ml (21 fl oz/2½ cups) cold water
1 teaspoon sesame oil

BEEF INTERCOSTALS WITH
KOREAN CHILLI DRESSING

Intercostal meat, also known as rib finger, is the meat found between ribs. It's not always readily available so it's a good idea to order it in advance from your butcher.

Trim the beef intercostals of any excess fat and sinew then place the meat in a baking dish just large enough to hold it in a single layer. Mix the sweet soy sauce through the beef and marinate in the refrigerator for 3 hours or overnight.

Preheat the oven to 150°C (300°F).

Fill the baking dish with the beef in it with just enough water to cover the meat. Cover the dish with foil and cook the beef in the oven for 3–4 hours until the meat is tender but not falling apart. Keep an eye on the water level and top up as necessary. When the meat is tender, allow it to cool in its liquid in the refrigerator.

To make the Korean chilli dressing, in a small bowl, mix all the ingredients together. Leave the sauce at room temperature for an hour before using, to let the flavour develop.

When you're ready to finish the dish, preheat a barbecue or chargrill pan to high.

Drain the beef and discard the liquid. Cut the beef into pieces roughly 6 cm (2½ in) long. When the grill is hot, brush the meat with a little grapeseed oil and cook the meat on the grill for 3 minutes on each side, or until the beef is charred and hot.

Remove the beef from the heat and season with salt. Arrange on a plate with the Korean dressing and a generous sprinkling of sesame seeds or fried shallots.

SERVES 6

1 kg (2 lb 3 oz) beef intercostals
60 ml (2 fl oz/¼ cup) sweet soy sauce
2 tablespoons grapeseed oil
toasted sesame seeds or Fried shallots (p.221) to serve

KOREAN CHILLI DRESSING
2 cm (¾ in) piece fresh ginger, finely grated
2 garlic cloves, finely grated
1 red Asian shallot, thinly sliced
2½ tablespoons Korean chilli flakes
2 tablespoons sesame seeds, toasted
2 tablespoons Korean fish sauce
2 tablespoons light soy sauce
2 tablespoons rice wine vinegar
60 ml (2 fl oz/¼ cup) grapeseed oil
3 teaspoons sesame oil

CHICKEN HEART AND THIGH
WITH YAKITORI SAUCE

I like to cook yakitori over hot binchotan coals. These are a Japanese charcoal, available online or in some grocery stores. I usually prepare the fire an hour before I plan on cooking the chicken. Soaking the chicken hearts in saltwater brine seasons them perfectly and makes for a juicier finish to the meat.

To make the yakitori sauce, bring all the ingredients to a simmer in a saucepan over medium heat. Reduce the heat to low and cook gently until it has reduced in volume by half. The sauce will be thick and glossy. Strain the sauce and set aside to cool to room temperature.

Stir the salt into 500 ml (17 fl oz/2 cups) water until the salt has dissolved. Add the chicken hearts to the brine and leave for 3 hours in the refrigerator to cure. At the same time, soak the bamboo skewers in water, which will stop them from burning on the grill.

Working with one skewer at a time, alternately thread 5 pieces of chicken thigh with 4 pieces of the spring onion, piercing the spring onion pieces perpendicular to the skewer. Brush with a little of the yakitori sauce and leave to marinate and dry in the refrigerator for 30 minutes.

Remove the chicken hearts from the brine and rinse them in cold water. Skewer the hearts and brush them with a little yakitori sauce. Leave them in the refrigerator for 30 minutes to marinate and dry.

Preheat a barbecue or chargrill pan to high.

Brush a little grapeseed oil over the chicken hearts and thighs and cook over the hot grill, turning every minute or so and brushing the top with sauce each time you turn until the chicken is cooked through and nicely glazed, 3–4 minutes.

SERVES 4

2½ tablespoons sea salt
300 g (10½ oz) cleaned chicken hearts
4 skinless, boneless chicken thighs,
   cut into 2 cm (¾ in) cubes
8 spring onions (scallions),
   white and pale green part only,
   cut into 2 cm (¾ in) pieces
bamboo skewers
2 tablespoons grapeseed oil

YAKITORI SAUCE

250 ml (8½ fl oz/1 cup) mirin
250 ml (8½ fl oz/1 cup) light soy sauce
125 ml (4 fl oz/½ cup) dry sake
2 tablespoons dark brown sugar
1 teaspoon black peppercorns
2 spring onions (scallions),
   white part only
2 garlic cloves, crushed
2 cm (¾ in) piece fresh ginger,
   thinly sliced

←
Bamboo stake through the hearts.

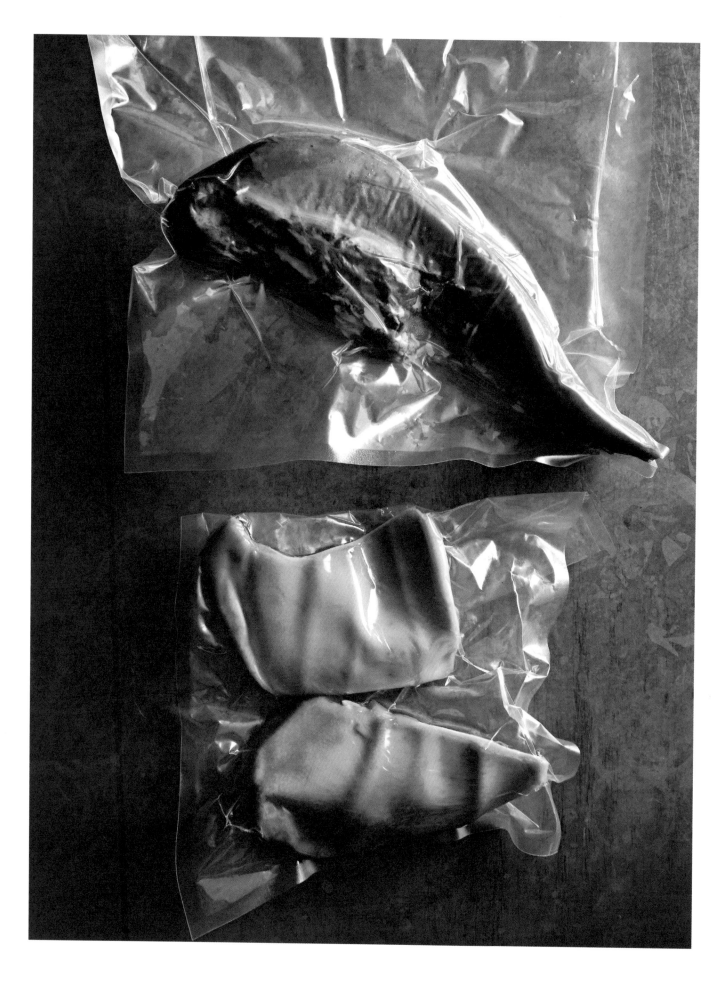

OX TONGUE, CRISP PIG'S EARS,
PICKLED CHILLI, FRIED GARLIC

This recipe is inspired by the sometimes challenging, but always delicious, offal (variety meat) cold cuts often found in restaurants in China.

Put the pig's ears and ox tongue in a large stockpot with the master stock ingredients and bring to a simmer over medium–low heat. Cook gently for 3 hours. Remove the tongue and ears from the stock. Reserve the stock and set aside.

While the tongue is still hot, peel off the outer skin and discard it. Place the ears and peeled tongue on a tray in the refrigerator until they are completely cold.

To make the fried garlic, in a large, heavy-based saucepan, heat the grapeseed oil to 140°C (275°F) or until a cube of bread dropped into the oil turns brown in 20 seconds. Set a fine sieve over another similar-sized pan and line a tray with paper towel.

Add the sliced garlic to the oil, stirring continuously. When the garlic chips are lightly golden, strain them through the sieve. Tip the garlic chips out onto the lined tray and use a fork to separate the chips and spread them out. Set aside to cool.

Take the pig's ears out of the refrigerator, slice them thinly and set aside. Cut the tongue into 1 cm (½ in) cubes.

Preheat the oven to 180°C (350°F).

Fill a large, heavy-based saucepan one-third full with vegetable oil and heat to 190°C (375°F) or until a cube of bread dropped into the oil turns brown in 15 seconds.

Toss the sliced pig's ears in a little flour to lightly coat them. Shake the excess flour off the slices and deep-fry them for 3 minutes or until crispy. Be careful, as they will spit. Transfer to paper towel to drain.

Place the tongue in a roasting tin with 2 tablespoons of the master stock, heat in the oven for 3 minutes or until warmed through. Transfer to a mixing bowl along with the cucumber and the pickled chilli and mix well. Place on a serving plate.

Mix the spring onion, coriander and pig's ears together and place them on top of the tongue. Crush over a small handful of the fried garlic and serve.

See photograph (p.91).

SERVES 6

2 pig's ears, cleaned
1 corned ox tongue, soaked overnight
  in water
vegetable oil for deep-frying
plain (all-purpose) flour for coating
1 baby cucumber, sliced into thin rounds
2 tablespoons Pickled chilli
  (p.220, but double the quantity
  of chillies)
2 spring onions (scallions),
  white part only, thinly sliced diagonally
¼ cup picked coriander (cilantro) leaves

MASTER STOCK

250 ml (8½ fl oz/1 cup) light soy sauce
1.5 litres (51 fl oz/6 cups) water
½ cup rock sugar
250 ml (8½ fl oz/1 cup) Shaoxing rice wine
20 g (¾ oz) fresh ginger, sliced
3 garlic cloves, sliced
1 spring onion (scallion),
  white part only, sliced
1 cinnamon stick
2 star anise
1 teaspoon white peppercorns

FRIED GARLIC

500 ml (17 fl oz/2 cups) grapeseed oil
20 garlic cloves, thinly sliced

↑
Tonkatsu sandwich construction: timing is everything.

↑
Ox tongue, crisp pig's ears, pickled chilli, fried garlic (p.89).

ROLLED PORK, WHITE KIMCHI,
YUXIANG SAUCE

The Yuxiang sauce recipe here will make twice as much sauce as you'll need but the remainder won't go to waste. It can last for a week in the refrigerator but will usually be eaten well before then. Any excess kimchi will keep well in the refrigerator for a few weeks, but alternatively simply halve the recipe.

To make the white kimchi, cut the Chinese cabbage in half, then cut each half into 5 x 2 cm (2 x ¾ in) pieces. Combine the 3 teaspoons sugar with the salt and mix well through the cabbage. Place the cabbage in a colander set over a bowl and leave for 24 hours.

Put the 2 tablespoons sugar in a small saucepan with 2 tablespoons water over medium heat and warm until the sugar has dissolved. Transfer to a food processor or blender with the garlic and the chopped ginger and process until smooth. Mix the paste with the remaining ingredients.

Squeeze the excess water out of the cabbage and place it in a bowl with the marinade, mixing thoroughly to combine. Place in a plastic container with a fitted lid and leave to ferment in the refrigerator for at least 1 week.

When ready to cook the pork, place a saucepan fitted with a steamer big enough to hold the pork belly on the stove and bring to a simmer. Steam the pork belly for 2½ hours or until tender.

Remove the pork belly from the steamer and cool overnight in the refrigerator, pressed between two plates lined with plastic wrap and weighted down with a few tins of food.

The following day, remove the skin from the pork and trim the edges of the meat so they're straight. Slice the belly as thinly as possible along the longest side.

Lay the slices of pork belly on a flat surface. Place 1 slice of chilli and 1 tablespoon of white kimchi at one end and then roll the pork belly around the kimchi. Place on a serving plate and spoon over the Yuxiang sauce. Drizzle with a little chilli oil and top with spring onion and coriander, if desired.

MAKES ABOUT 15 ROLLS
1 kg (2 lb 3 oz) piece pork belly, skin on
1 green bird's eye chilli, thinly sliced
Yuxiang sauce (p.218)
1 tablespoon chilli oil
1 spring onion (scallion), thinly sliced
  (optional)
¼ cup picked coriander (cilantro) leaves
  (optional)

WHITE KIMCHI
1 Chinese cabbage (wombok)
2 tablespoons sugar, plus 3 teaspoons
  extra
1 tablespoon sea salt
3 garlic cloves
thumb-sized piece fresh ginger,
  chopped, plus thumb-sized piece
  fresh ginger, julienned
250 ml (8½ fl oz/1 cup) light soy sauce
250 ml (8½ fl oz/1 cup) rice vinegar
1 carrot, julienned
3 spring onions (scallions), thinly sliced

↑↑
Tim orchestrating the dinner service.
↑
Coveted seat at the kitchen bar.

Tonkatsu refers to crumbed and deep-fried pork cutlet. In specialist tonkatsu restaurants in Japan, you are given a choice between various grades of pork before it is crumbed and fried. Often the pork is served on its own with a garnish of shredded cabbage and a bowl of the house special tonkatsu sauce. Another popular way is to serve the fried pork in a simple sandwich of 'fake' white bread. Indulgent, and incredibly delicious!

To make the tonkatsu sauce, combine all the ingredients in a large saucepan. Bring the mixture to the boil and then reduce the heat to a simmer. Cook gently for 20 minutes, stirring occasionally with a wooden spoon. Remove from the heat and leave to cool to room temperature. Purée the sauce in a blender or food processor or with a hand-held blender, before passing it through a fine sieve.

Lightly season the pork slices with sea salt and refrigerate for 10 minutes.

Place the flour, egg and breadcrumbs in separate shallow bowls.

Remove the pork from the refrigerator and pat dry with paper towel. To crumb, dip a piece of the pork loin first in the flour, then in the beaten egg and finally in the breadcrumb mixture, pressing so that the crumbs adhere. Repeat this process with each piece of pork and return the crumbed pork to the refrigerator.

In a shallow frying pan heat the grapeseed oil over medium heat. When hot add two of the pork loins and cook until golden, about 3 minutes. Turn the pork loins over and continue to cook for a further 3 minutes or until golden, adding more oil if necessary. Remove the cooked pork and repeat the process with the other 2 crumbed pork loins.

Lightly butter each slice of bread and spread 4 slices with 1 teaspoon each of tonkatsu sauce. Season the pork and place it on the bread. Top each piece of pork with 1 teaspoon of tonkatsu sauce and the remaining slices of bread.

Place a plate on each sandwich to gently press down on the sandwiches. Leave the plate on the sandwiches for 30 seconds to 'set' them.

Remove the crusts and slice the sandwiches in half. Serve immediately.

SERVES 4

400 g (14 oz) pork loin, skin off
  and sliced into 4 even slices
sea salt
35 g (1¼ oz/¼ cup) plain
  (all-purpose) flour
2 eggs, lightly beaten
60 g (2 oz/1 cup) panko breadcrumbs
80 ml (2½ fl oz/⅓ cup) grapeseed oil
8 slices thick-cut white bread
40 g (1½ oz) butter, softened

TONKATSU SAUCE

½ onion, finely chopped
1.5 cm (½ in) piece fresh ginger, grated
1 garlic clove, crushed
3 carrots, finely chopped
1 celery stalk, finely chopped
½ granny smith apple, peeled and grated
90 ml (3 fl oz) tomato sauce (ketchup)
70 ml (2¼ fl oz) Worcestershire sauce
80 ml (2½ fl oz/⅓ cup) rice wine vinegar
2½ tablespoons mirin
¼ teaspoon ground allspice
pinch of ground cinnamon
pinch of ground cloves
55 g (2 oz/¼ cup firmly packed)
  brown sugar
1 teaspoon Dijon mustard
100 ml (3½ fl oz) water

GRILLED OCTOPUS
WITH FERMENTED CHILLI

This is an easy method of cooking octopus that never fails. It can be applied to many octopus recipes, not just this one.

Rinse the octopus tentacles and pat them dry, but do not remove the skin or suckers.

Heat the grapeseed oil in a large non-reactive saucepan with a tight-fitting lid over medium heat. Sauté the tentacles for a few minutes in the hot oil to seal them on all sides. Add 125 ml (4 fl oz/½ cup) water, reduce the heat to low and cover with the lid. Cook until the octopus is tender, up to 45 minutes, shifting it about with tongs from time to time so it cooks evenly. Remove the pan from the heat and allow to cool slightly. Keep the octopus in the cooking liquid until you are ready to use it.

When you wish to serve the octopus remove it from the liquid and pat dry. Brush the tentacles with a little oil and season with a pinch of salt. Preheat you grill or bbq and cook the octopus until the skin has lightly caramelised and is gently charred.

Cut the octopus into manageable sizes and lengths and arrange it on a serving plate. Finish the dish with small amounts of fermented chilli dotted on and around the octopus.

See photograph (p.101).

SERVES 6
1 kg (2 lb 3 oz) octopus tentacles
60 ml (2 fl oz/¼ cup) grapeseed oil, plus extra for basting
sea salt
Fermented chilli (p.221) to serve

↑
Setting up.
→
Grilled octopus with fermented chilli (p.99).

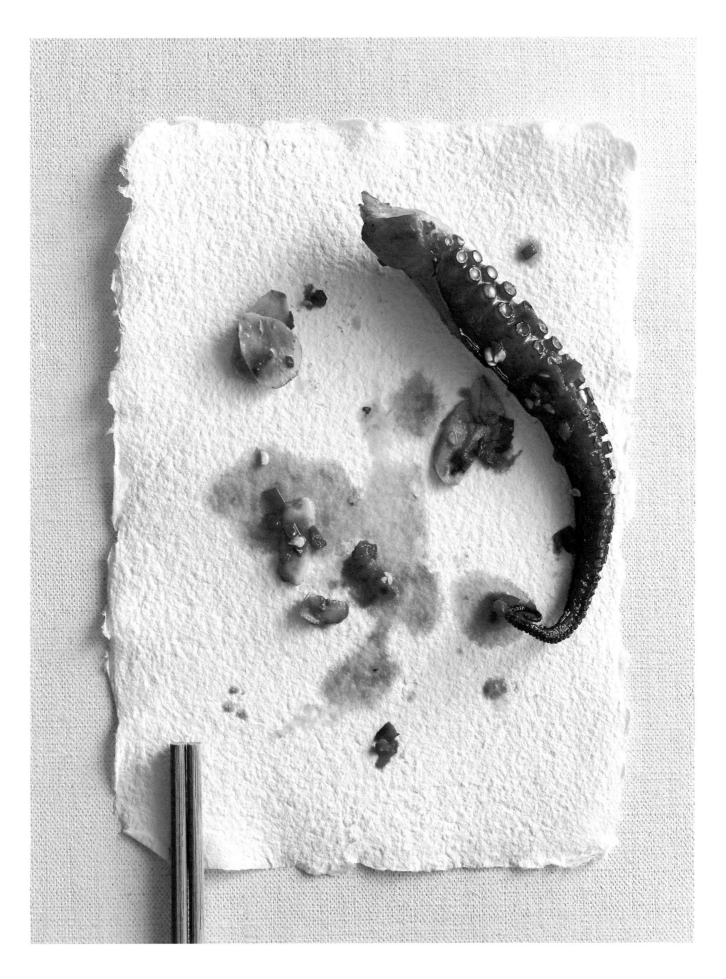

I like to serve this with a small bowl of XO sauce (p.218) on the side.

Place the rice in a stainless steel saucepan and cover with 1 cm (½ in) cold water. Bring to a simmer over medium–high heat, stirring occasionally, then reduce the heat to low, cover the saucepan and cook until just tender, about 10–12 minutes. Turn the heat off, remove the lid and cover the pan with a tea (dish) towel. Let the rice stand for 5 minutes before spreading it out on a tray to cool. At this stage the rice should be cooked and loose. If it seems gluey and wet, discard it and start again.

Heat the oil in a large wok or non-stick frying pan over medium–high heat. Add the spring onion and garlic and cook until the garlic is fragrant. Add the egg mix and swirl it around the pan as if making a crêpe. Scatter the cooled rice over the egg and mix it in with a wooden spoon, breaking up the egg as you do. Add the soy sauce, mustard greens and sugar. Stir the rice continuously until it is coated with soy sauce and egg.

Gently toss the crabmeat through the rice just before serving and finish with the white pepper and sesame seeds.

SERVES 2

220 g (8 oz/1 cup) short-grain
    Japanese rice, rinsed
2 tablespoons grapeseed oil
2 spring onions (scallions),
    white part only, thinly sliced
½ garlic clove, finely chopped
1 egg plus 1 egg white,
    lightly beaten together
2 teaspoons light soy sauce
1 tablespoon finely chopped pickled
    mustard greens
pinch of caster (superfine) sugar
150–200 g (5½–7 oz) picked,
    cooked spanner (or mud) crabmeat
pinch of ground white pepper
pinch of toasted sesame seeds

SPANNER CRAB SALAD, CABBAGE HEART, MISO DRESSING, NORI

To make the nori powder, preheat the oven to 120°C (250°F) and line a baking tray with baking paper.

Place the nori, kombu and puffed wild rice on the baking tray. Turn the oven off and place the tray in the oven. Warm gently in the residual heat for 3–5 minutes until aromatic and slightly crisp. Remove from the oven and cool to room temperature.

Pulse the nori and kombu to a fine powder in a spice grinder, ensuring there are no large pieces. Add the puffed rice and blitz until you have a coarse crumb. Season with the salt and store in an airtight container.

Bring a small saucepan of water to the boil. Add the egg and boil for 8 minutes, then cool in a bowl of iced water. Peel the egg, then separate the white from the yolk. Discard the yolk, finely chop the egg white and set it aside.

Remove the green outer leaves from the Chinese cabbage. Tear the white and yellow cabbage heart into small pieces — you will need about 1½ cups of cabbage for the salad. Wash the cabbage and dry well.

Transfer the cabbage to a bowl with the watercress and 2 tablespoons of the miso dressing and toss gently to combine. Taste and add more dressing if necessary.

Arrange the dressed cabbage on a plate and scatter the diced nashi and egg white over the cabbage.

In a separate bowl, lightly season the crabmeat with the remaining miso dressing and salt to taste. Strew the seasoned crabmeat over the salad and season with plenty of the nori powder.

SERVES 4

1 egg
½ Chinese cabbage (wombok)
½ cup picked watercress leaves
3 tablespoons Miso dressing (p.219)
1 nashi, peeled and diced
150 g (5½ oz) picked, cooked spanner (or mud) crabmeat
sea salt

NORI POWDER

5 g (¼ oz) nori sheets, torn into small pieces
10 g (¼ oz) shaved tororo kombu
20 g (¾ oz) puffed wild rice
½ teaspoon salt

SHAVED CUTTLEFISH, MUSSELS, BLACK PEPPER SAUCE, PICKLED CHILLI

You can substitute calamari for the cuttlefish in this recipe without compromising the finished dish.

To make the master pickle liquid, combine the vinegar, 125 ml (4 fl oz/½ cup) water, the sugar and salt in a stainless steel saucepan and heat until the sugar has dissolved, taking care not to let it boil. Remove from the heat and let it cool for 5 minutes before using.

Bring a large saucepan of water to the boil. Season the water with a good pinch of salt.

Put the cuttlefish in a bowl and pour the boiling water over it. Stir the cuttlefish around to separate the slices and strain it after 20 seconds. Drain the cuttlefish on paper towel then lay the slices out flat and place in the refrigerator to cool.

Using a peeler or a mandoline, shave off thin slices from the celery stalk. Submerge the celery shavings in the master pickle liquid and leave for 10 minutes.

Meanwhile steam the mussels for 3 minutes or until they have all opened. Leave them to cool for a few minutes then remove them from their shells and cut them in half. Place them in a bowl with the cuttlefish, jicama, pickled celery, spring onion, black pepper sauce and a pinch of sea salt. Leave to marinate for 5 minutes.

Arrange the salad on a serving plate, top with the pickled chilli and red-veined sorrel (if using) and serve.

SERVES 4

sea salt
125 g (4½ oz) cleaned cuttlefish,
    thinly sliced diagonally
1 celery stalk, cut into 5 cm (2 in) lengths
125 ml (4 fl oz/½ cup) master pickle liquid
    (see method)
12 mussels
½ jicama, peeled and diced
1 spring onion (scallion),
    white part only, thinly sliced
70 ml (2¼ fl oz) Black pepper sauce (p.218)
6 red-veined sorrel leaves (optional)
Pickled chilli (p.220)

MASTER PICKLE LIQUID
60 ml (2 fl oz/¼ cup) rice wine vinegar
2 tablespoons sugar
2 teaspoons salt

↑
Supplier bounty.

PIPIS, XO SAUCE, FRIED BREAD

My absolute favourite thing to eat, full stop. Pipis and XO sauce is the late-night dish of choice for chefs everywhere. It's packed full of rich flavours and is an interactive, social way to eat. A pot of pipis is a celebration. The addition of fried bread adds a great texture and is also useful for mopping up the sauce. Fried bread is available at most Asian grocery stores.

Preheat the oven to 180°C (350°F).

Bake the fried bread for 3 minutes until crisp. Slice each piece of bread into 1 cm (½ in) thick pieces and set aside.

Put the pipis and a splash of water In a large saucepan or wok over high heat. Cover the saucepan with a lid. Check the pipis after 1 minute, stirring them vigorously before replacing the lid. Repeat until most of the pipis have opened. Drain the pipis and reserve the cooking liquid.

In a separate saucepan, fry the XO sauce over medium–high heat until aromatic. Add the opened clams and 60 ml (2 fl oz/¼ cup) of the reserved cooking liquid to the pan, stirring vigorously over the heat for 1 minute. Add the lemon juice and adjust the seasoning if needed.

Finally, mix the fried bread through the pipis. Continue to stir until coated. Transfer to a serving bowl and serve immediately.

SERVES 6

3 sticks fried bread (Chinese doughnuts)
2 kg (4 lb 6 oz) pipis or small clams (vongole)
60 ml (2 fl oz/¼ cup) XO sauce (p.218)
2 teaspoons lemon juice

SCHOOL PRAWNS,
ICEBERG LETTUCE, KIMCHI

Preheat the oven to 60°C (140°F) and line a baking tray with baking paper.

Spread the kimchi cabbage leaves flat on the tray and dehydrate them in the oven for 5 hours or until dry (or in a dehydrator for 2 hours).

When you are ready to serve the prawns, heat the grapeseed oil in a large frying pan over high heat. Sauté the prawns for 2 minutes or until just cooked — the shell should be crisp. Season with a pinch of salt.

Place the shredded iceberg lettuce on a serving plate, arranging the prawns over the top. Dot the mayonnaise on and around the prawns. Roughly break the cabbage into shards and arrange it among the prawns. Sprinkle the whole plate with shichimi togarashi and serve.

SERVES 4

3 large cabbage leaves from
  the Kimchi recipe (p.219)
1 tablespoon grapeseed oil
200 g (7 oz) raw whole school
  prawns (shrimp)
sea salt
¼ iceberg lettuce, shredded
2 tablespoons Kewpie mayonnaise
1 teaspoon shichimi togarashi
  (Japanese chilli powder)

I like to serve this quick, refreshing appetiser in summer.
The highlight for me is the texture of the cold udon noodles.

To make the soy dashi, wipe the kombu with a damp cloth to clean it.

In a saucepan over medium heat, put the kombu and shiitake mushrooms
in the room temperature water. Heat it to 60°C (140°F) — you should start
seeing steam. Remove the pan from the heat and leave it to steep for
1 hour. Strain and discard the kombu and shiitake mushrooms and return
the liquid to the pan.

Heat the liquid to 80°C (175°F) — you should start seeing a few bubbles
in the water. Remove the pan from the heat and add the bonito flakes.
Leave the bonito to infuse for 5 minutes. Strain the stock, resisting the
temptation to press on the bonito to get all the stock out — this will make
the stock go cloudy. Season the dashi with the soy sauce and leave in
the refrigerator to cool.

Slice the spring onions thinly on an angle then place them in a small bowl
of iced water to curl.

Bring a large saucepan of water to the boil, add the udon noodles and
cook according to the instructions on the packet. Strain the noodles
and put them in a colander along with a cup of ice cubes to cool down.
Gently toss the noodles through the ice to cool. When cool, remove the
ice from the noodles and strain them well. Toss the drained noodles in
a bowl with the sesame oil and soy sauce.

When serving, divide the noodles between four bowls and top each with
some spring onion and a slice of pickled shiitake mushroom. Pour the
dashi over the noodles and serve with the shichimi togarashi and sesame
seeds sprinkled over.

SERVES 4

2 spring onions (scallions)
150 g (5½ oz) dried udon noodles
1 teaspoon sesame oil
1 tablespoon soy sauce
2 Pickled shiitake mushrooms (p.59),
  thinly sliced
shichimi togarashi
  (Japanese chilli powder)

SOY DASHI

15 g (½ oz) kombu
2 dried shiitake mushrooms,
  soaked in water for 10 minutes
750 ml (25½ fl oz/3 cups) water,
  room temperature (20–30°C/68–86°F)
9 g (¼ oz) bonito flakes (katsuobushi)
60 ml (2 fl oz/¼ cup) light soy sauce

This is not a traditional ramen whatsoever. We have taken the basic principles of ramen and created our own version, which we serve at lunchtime. Traditionally, ramen stock is made from pork and can be quite rich. I prefer a lighter-style broth, which is the reason I use a chicken stock here.

To make the soy eggs, in a small saucepan bring all the ingredients, except the eggs, to a simmer. Cook over low heat for 5 minutes. Add 500 ml (17 fl oz/2 cups) cold water, remove the pan from the heat and set aside.

Bring a saucepan of water to the boil. Pierce a small hole in the larger end of each egg using a thin metal skewer.

Carefully put the eggs in the boiling water and cook for exactly 6 minutes, stirring slowly for the first 1½ minutes to distribute the heat evenly.

Meanwhile, fill a large bowl with cold water and ice. When the eggs are done, transfer them straight to the ice bath and leave to cool for 15 minutes.

Once the eggs are cool, peel them in the water — this will help them keep a perfect exterior. Transfer the eggs to the soy sauce mixture and marinate in the refrigerator for at least 2 and up to 6 hours, making sure they're completely submerged in the liquid by placing a small plate on top of them.

To serve, take the eggs out of the marinade and cut them in half lengthways. The soy sauce mixture can be reserved for another batch of eggs. (The eggs will keep, refrigerated in a tightly sealed container, for up to a month.)

To make the ramen broth, preheat the oven to 220°C (430°F).

Chop the chicken wings into 3 cm (1¼ in) pieces with a cleaver. Put them in an ovenproof dish and roast for 30 minutes or until golden brown.

Heat a chargrill pan over high heat. Cook the carrot and onion for 10 minutes on one side until well charred.

Put all the broth ingredients, except the soy sauce, in a large stainless steel stockpot and bring to a simmer. Simmer for 2 hours to develop the flavours. Strain the stock through a fine sieve and add the soy sauce.

SERVES 4

2 tablespoons grapeseed oil
2 boneless chicken thighs, skin on
8 Prawn and chicken dumplings (p.125) (optional)
500 g (1 lb 2 oz) ramen noodles (buy fresh noodles from a Japanese grocer)
2 spring onions (scallions), green tops only, thinly sliced diagonally
1 tablespoon shichimi togarashi (Japanese chilli powder)
1 tablespoon sesame seeds, toasted and coarsely ground
2 sheets toasted nori, each cut into 6 squares

SOY EGGS

2 tablespoons sake
2 tablespoons mirin
4 garlic cloves, thinly sliced
3 cm (1¼ in) piece fresh ginger, thinly sliced
190 ml (6½ fl oz/¾ cup) light soy sauce
2 tablespoons caster (superfine) sugar
4 eggs

RAMEN BROTH

600 g (1 lb 5 oz) chicken wings
½ carrot
1 onion
2 litres (68 fl oz/8 cups) light chicken stock
10 x 5 cm (4 x 2 in) piece kombu
¼ cup white miso paste
4 dried shiitake mushrooms
1 celery stalk
3 cm (1¼ in) piece fresh ginger
2 tomatoes, peeled and roughly chopped
2 tablespoons light soy sauce

In a saucepan over medium heat, bring the strained ramen broth
to a simmer. Reduce the heat to low.

Heat the grapeseed oil in a non-stick frying pan over low heat. Place the
chicken thighs, skin side down, in the pan and cook gently for 5 minutes,
or until golden. Turn the chicken over and cook for a further 2 minutes,
or until cooked through. Remove the chicken from the pan and slice each
thigh into 8 pieces.

Meanwhile, bring a large saucepan of water to the boil. Carefully drop
in the dumplings (if using) and cook for 2 minutes. Drop the noodles into
the same pot and cook with the dumplings for a further 3 minutes.
Strain through a colander.

Divide the noodles and dumplings between four bowls. Place 1 egg and
4 slices of chicken in each bowl, then divide the hot broth among the
bowls. Top with the spring onion greens and sprinkle with a combination
of shichimi togarashi and ground sesame seeds. Finally, tuck 3 squares
of toasted nori into the side of the bowl and serve.

See photograph (p.115).

Supernormal ramen (p.112).

I've never met anyone who doesn't love dumplings. They seem to appeal to every demographic and are incredibly satisfying to eat — the combination of flavour, texture and convenience, plus the social aspect of sharing dumplings hit all the right pleasure buttons.

Dumplings are among the most popular items on the menu at Supernormal and we have two dedicated dumpling chefs who make up to 2000 of them per day. When I lived in Hong Kong I ate them almost every day and learned how to make them from some of the guys I worked with there. Since then I've made them at home very regularly but I've never made dumplings or used steamed bread in any of my other restaurants prior to Supernormal.

There's a method and a technique to dumplings and to bao that you can't mess with too much but at the same time you can explore new ideas for fillings. Our potsticker dumpling is traditional Shanghainese but our prawn and chicken dumplings and the pig's head bao are recipes that have evolved over time in the Supernormal kitchen.

I really like the social aspect of making dumplings at home with children or with friends but people are often intimidated by the idea of making dumplings because they've never done it before. So when I have people around for dinner I'll make a dumpling mix beforehand and keep it in the refrigerator. If my friends ask if they can give me a hand with anything, I pull it out and give them a lesson on how to make the dumplings and let them do the rest. Most people are surprised by how quickly they pick it up and love doing it, though I do also have some friends who have now stopped asking me if they can help with anything when they come over for dinner.

Bring a large saucepan of water to the boil. Blanch the spinach for 10 seconds and then cool immediately in iced water. Place the cold spinach in a colander, squeezing it in your hands to remove all the excess liquid. Roughly chop the spinach and set aside.

Heat the grapeseed oil in a small frying pan over medium heat and cook the garlic chives and spring onion for a few seconds until aromatic. Add the tofu and cook for 3 minutes. Add the preserved vegetable and spinach and cook for 2 more minutes, then season with the sea salt and white pepper. Remove from the heat and allow to cool. Once cool, stir through the sesame oil and adjust the seasoning if necessary.

To make the dumplings, place a rounded teaspoon of the filling in the centre of a wonton wrapper. Dip your finger in water and moisten the bottom edge of the wrapper. Gather the points of the wrapper up around the filling to form a pouch. Squeeze the wrapper together at the top to seal the dumpling. Repeat with the remaining filling and wrappers.

Put the finished dumplings on a tray dusted lightly with flour and store them in the refrigerator until ready to use.

Slice the ginger into a super-fine julienne and leave to steep in cold water until ready to use.

Cook the dumplings, in batches if necessary, for 4 minutes in a large saucepan of boiling water. Remove the dumplings with a slotted spoon and drain.

Serve a few dumplings per person in a bowl. Top each bowl of dumplings with some ginger shreds, 1 teaspoon soy sauce and ½ teaspoon garlic oil.

MAKES ABOUT 20 DUMPLINGS

600 g (1 lb 5 oz) English spinach, washed
1 tablespoon grapeseed oil
3 tablespoons thinly sliced flowering garlic chives
2 spring onions (scallions), white part only, thinly sliced
150 g (5½ oz) firm tofu, finely chopped
80 g (2¾ oz) Chinese preserved vegetable, finely chopped
½ teaspoon sea salt
½ teaspoon ground white pepper
1 teaspoon sesame oil
1 packet wonton wrappers
plain (all-purpose) flour for dusting
5 cm (2 in) piece fresh ginger
Garlic oil (p.219) to serve
soy sauce to serve

This is a very traditional Shanghai dumpling and the closest we serve at Supernormal to a purely authentic dumpling.

Toss the cabbage with the salt and leave it in a colander for 15 minutes to wilt. Squeeze out all excess liquid until dry.

Combine the salted cabbage with the egg yolk, spring onion, garlic chives, garlic, ginger, pork, soy sauce, sesame oil, pepper, sugar, potato starch, stock and five-spice in a bowl and mix well — it's easiest to work the ingredients into the pork by hand.

To form the dumplings, place 1½–2 teaspoons of the filling in the centre of a wrapper. Lightly wet one edge of the wrapper, fold the dough over and firmly pinch the edges together. Lay the dumplings on a floured tray until ready to cook.

Combine the flour with 200 ml (7 fl oz) water, whisking well.

Heat the oil in a non-stick frying pan with a fitted lid over medium heat. Place 6 dumplings in the pan. Fry for 1 minute then add 60 ml (2 fl oz/¼ cup) of the flour and water mixture to the pan. Put the lid on and steam for 3 minutes. Remove the lid and cook for a further 5–8 minutes until the dumplings are cooked through and their bottoms are golden. Carefully loosen the dumplings and crust and flip them onto a plate.

Serve with small bowls of Chinese black vinegar for dipping.

MAKES ABOUT 20 DUMPLINGS

150 g (5½ oz/2 cups) thinly sliced baby Chinese cabbage (wombok)
1 tablespoon salt
1 egg yolk
15 g (½ oz/¼ cup) thinly sliced spring onions (scallions), white part only
20 g (¾ oz/⅓ cup) finely chopped garlic chives
2 garlic cloves, finely chopped
1 tablespoon finely chopped fresh ginger
300 g (10½ oz) minced (ground) pork
125 ml (4 fl oz/½ cup) light soy sauce
2 tablespoons sesame oil
¼ teaspoon freshly ground black pepper
1 teaspoon sugar
2 tablespoons potato starch
60 ml (2 fl oz/¼ cup) chicken stock
¼ teaspoon Chinese five-spice
1 packet round Shanghai (flour and water) dumpling wrappers or gyoza wrappers
1 tablespoon plain (all-purpose) flour
60 ml (2 fl oz/¼ cup) vegetable oil
2 tablespoons Chinese black vinegar to serve

This makes for a delicious item more like a large bun than a dumpling. We have from time to time replaced the oxtail with wagyu shin, which brings its own distinct flavour. It's best to cook the oxtail the day before you plan to make these dumplings.

Preheat the oven to 150°C (300°F).

To make a sauce, in a small saucepan over medium heat, gently cook 1 teaspoon of the grapeseed oil, add the chilli bean paste and sauté for 10 seconds. Add the Shaoxing rice wine and let it reduce for a minute before adding the rock sugar, chicken stock, five-spice and sea salt. Cook until the sugar has dissolved. Remove from the heat and set aside.

In a large saucepan warm 30 ml (1 fl oz) of the grapeseed oil over high heat. Season the oxtail with salt and sear the oxtail until browned all over. Transfer to a heavy roasting dish and pour over the sauce along with 250 ml (8½ fl oz/1 cup) water. Cover the tray tightly with foil, then place it in the oven and roast for 2 hours.

Reduce the heat to 110°C (230°F) and cook for a further 4 hours. Check every so often and turn the pieces of oxtail over, adding a little more water if the dish is getting a bit dry. Remove from the oven and leave to cool to room temperature. When cool, remove the pieces of oxtail and pick the meat from the bones. Reserve the braising liquid.

Meanwhile in a saucepan over medium heat, gently cook the onion in 1 teaspoon grapeseed oil until translucent. Add the reserved braising liquid and reduce until very thick and sticky.

Place the picked meat in a large bowl and add the spring onion along with 60 ml (2 fl oz/¼ cup) of the reduced cooking liquid. Mix well and season with the white pepper and a squeeze of lemon juice. Taste and add more of the reduced cooking liquid if it seems too dry.

Spread out onto a tray and place in the refrigerator to cool.

Preheat the oven to 190°C (375°F).

To make the hot water pastry, in a bowl mix together both flours and the salt. Make a well in the centre and add the boiling water, followed by the room temperature water, mixing until the dough comes together. Add the lard and continue to mix until well combined and smooth. Portion the dough into 40 g (1½ oz) balls.

MAKES ABOUT 10 DUMPLINGS
60 ml (2 fl oz/¼ cup) grapeseed oil
1 tablespoon chilli bean paste
80 ml (2½ fl oz/⅓ cup) Shaoxing
   rice wine
1 tablespoon rock sugar
250 ml (8½ fl oz/1 cup) chicken stock
2 tablespoons Chinese five-spice
2 teaspoons sea salt
1 kg (2 lb 3 oz) oxtail, cut into
   2 cm (¾ in) pieces
½ onion, finely diced
2 spring onions (scallions),
   white part only, thinly sliced
pinch of ground white pepper
juice of ½ lemon

HOT WATER PASTRY
30 g (1 oz) bread flour, sifted
120 g (4½ oz) plain
   (all-purpose) flour, sifted
½ teaspoon salt
100 ml (3½ fl oz) boiling water
1 tablespoon water, at room
   temperature (20–30°C/68–86°F)
1 teaspoon lard

On a lightly floured surface, roll the dough out using the 'turn and roll' technique to make the edges thinner and to leave the middle thicker. Spoon 40 g (1½ oz) of the oxtail mix onto a piece of dough and enclose the pastry around it making it into a flat disc. Repeat with the remaining dough. Refrigerate the dumplings for 2–3 hours before cooking.

To cook the dumplings, gently warm the remaining grapeseed oil in an ovenproof frying pan over medium heat and place the dumplings in the pan, fold side down. Cook for 2 minutes or until golden, then carefully turn over and cook the other side for 30 seconds. Transfer the pan to the oven and bake for 4 minutes or until nice and golden. Serve immediately.

↑
Pan-frying dumplings.

PRAWN AND CHICKEN DUMPLINGS
WITH SPICED VINEGAR

We serve up to 2000 dumplings a day at Supernormal and these prawn and chicken numbers, our riff on a traditional Chinese recipe, are one of our bestsellers. The spiced vinegar recipe makes more than you will need for the dumplings, but it keeps well in the refrigerator and can be used to enliven all sorts of Chinese dishes.

In a bowl, combine the prawns with the egg white, ¼ teaspoon of the salt, the tapioca and bicarbonate of soda and place in the refrigerator to marinate for 1 hour.

To make the spiced vinegar, toast the spices in a small, dry frying pan over medium heat until fragrant. Add 200 ml (7 fl oz) water and bring to the boil. Boil until reduced by half. Set aside to cool. When cool, strain and discard the spices. Stir in the remaining ingredients and set aside.

Heat the grapeseed oil in a small saucepan over medium heat and cook the garlic chives for 1 minute then scrape them into a bowl to cool.

Take the prawns from the refrigerator and coarsely dice one-third of them. Finely chop the remainder of the prawns into a mince. Mix the prawn and chicken mince together and combine them by repeatedly throwing the mixture against the inside of the mixing bowl. It will become a sticky, cohesive mass. This strengthens the protein to give the mixture a firmer texture. Finally add the garlic chives, sesame oil, sugar, remaining salt, the fish sauce, soy sauce and white pepper. Thoroughly mix these ingredients through the mince.

To make the dumplings, place a rounded teaspoon of the filling in the centre of a wonton wrapper. Dip your finger in water and moisten the bottom edge of the wrapper. Fold the wrapper in half towards you, to enclose the filling. Press to seal.

Fold the sealed edge of the wonton back on itself then lightly moisten one corner of the folded edge with water. Finally, taking the 2 ends in your fingers, bring them together with a twisting action, and press them firmly to join. Repeat with the remaining filling and wrappers.

Cook the dumplings in batches for 4 minutes in a large saucepan of boiling water. Remove them with a slotted spoon and drain. Serve immediately with some spiced vinegar spooned over the top.

MAKES ABOUT 20 DUMPLINGS

250 g (9 oz) peeled, raw prawns (shrimp), deveined
1 teaspoon egg white
½ teaspoon salt
½ teaspoon tapioca starch
¼ teaspoon bicarbonate of soda (baking soda)
1 teaspoon grapeseed oil
250 g (9 oz) minced (ground) chicken
1 tablespoon finely chopped garlic chives
¼ teaspoon sesame oil
pinch of sugar
¼ teaspoon fish sauce
1½ teaspoons soy sauce
pinch of ground white pepper
1 packet yellow wonton wrappers

SPICED VINEGAR

1 star anise
¼ teaspoon coriander seeds
½ cinnamon stick
2 cloves
70 ml (2¼ fl oz) Chinese black vinegar
70 ml (2¼ fl oz) tablespoons soy sauce
1½ tablespoons sugar
30 g (1 oz/½ cup) thinly sliced spring onion (scallion)
125 ml (4 fl oz/½ cup) chilli crisp sauce (we use Lao Gan Ma brand)

↑
Start of the day.

↑
Lao Gan Ma brand chilli crisp sauce.

↑
Troy the butcher from Meatsmith.

STEAMED PORK BUNS WITH
CHILLI VINEGAR DRESSING

To make the braised pork, preheat the oven to 150°C (300°F).

Place the pork belly, skin side up, in a roasting tin.

Combine the ginger, soy sauce and peppercorns and rub the mixture all over the pork. Add the chicken stock and bake the pork until very tender, approximately 2½ hours. Leave to cool to room temperature.

Once cool, remove the pork from the stock and place it on a tray. Weigh the pork down with a heavy plate and refrigerate until firm.

Once firm, remove the skin and cut the pork into 5 x 1 cm (2 x ½ in) slices. Set aside.

To make the buns, in a bowl combine the steamed buns cake flour and sugar. Using your hand, mix the flour and sugar while slowly adding the milk and oil to form a dough. Knead the dough for 3–4 minutes on a work surface until it is smooth and elastic. Divide the dough into 12 equal pieces and roll each piece into a ball. Place the dough balls on a tray and leave to rest in the refrigerator for 30 minutes.

On a lightly floured work surface, roll the dough balls into 10 cm (4 in) rounds. Place one piece of pork belly in the middle of each circle of dough. Lightly brush the edges of the dough with water then pull the dough up over the top of the pork belly to enclose it. Pinch the dough together to seal the dumpling.

As you make them, place the buns on a tray lined with baking paper and leave them in the refrigerator until all the dumplings are finished.

When you wish to serve the dumplings, bring a large saucepan of water fitted with a steamer to the boil. Place the dumplings in the steamer, sealed side down, and steam over rapidly boiling water until the dumplings rise, approximately 12–15 minutes.

To make the chilli vinegar dressing, combine all the ingredients in a bowl and set aside.

Serve the pork buns with the chilli vinegar dressing.

MAKES 12 BUNS

BUNS
450 g (1 lb) Rooster brand
  steamed bun cake flour
115 g (4 oz/½ cup) caster (superfine) sugar
250 ml (8½ fl oz/1 cup) milk
1 teaspoon grapeseed oil

BRAISED PORK
1 kg (2 lb 3 oz) piece boneless pork belly
8 cm (3¼ in) piece fresh ginger,
  thinly sliced
80 ml (2½ fl oz/⅓ cup) light soy sauce
6 white peppercorns, crushed
500 ml (17 fl oz/2 cups) chicken stock

CHILLI VINEGAR DRESSING
2 tablespoons black bean chilli sauce
1 tablespoon Chinese black vinegar
½ tablespoon light soy sauce
½ tablespoon water

↑
Dan Chan steaming buns.
→
Pig's head bao with chilli tamarind dressing (p.132).

PIG'S HEAD BAO WITH
CHILLI TAMARIND DRESSING

We have chef David Thompson to thank for the chilli tamarind sauce recipe, which is now indispensable in our kitchen. Braised and sliced pork jowl or belly is a worthy (and simpler) replacement for the pig's head.

To make the pressed pig's head, combine the five-spice and salt and sprinkle this mixture over the pig's head. Place on a rack in a baking dish and leave overnight in the refrigerator.

Place a saucepan fitted with a steamer on the stove and bring to a simmer over medium heat. Place the pig's head in the steamer and cook for 3 hours. Remove from the steamer and, when the head is cool enough to handle, remove as much of the meat, skin and fat as possible, apart from the eyes. The head should yield approximately 1 kg (2 lb 3 oz) meat.

Thinly slice the ear. Peel the tongue and roughly chop it along with the rest of the flesh.

In a large bowl, mix the meat well with the remaining ingredients. Taste to check the seasoning.

Line a 20 x 10 cm (8 x 4 in) deep tray with plastic wrap. Press the prepared head meat into the tray. Cover with plastic wrap and cover with another tray the same size. Chill in the refrigerator until very firm. Once set, cut the meat into 2.5 cm (1 in) squares.

To make the chilli tamarind dressing, heat a chargrill pan until hot. Place the fresh chillies on the grill, turning them until nicely charred. Next grill the dried chillies. Seed the fresh chillies and roughly chop them with the dried chillies. Set aside.

In a medium saucepan over medium–low heat, gently warm the grapeseed oil. Add the shallots and garlic and cook for 3–4 minutes until aromatic and wilted. Add the chilli and cook until aromatic. Transfer the shallots and chillies to a blender along with the coriander, scud chillies, tamarind, sugar, fish sauce, 2 tablespoons water and the lime juice. Blend the sauce until completely smooth. Set aside.

Put the flour, egg and breadcrumbs in three separate shallow bowls. Dip the pork squares first in the flour, then in the beaten egg and finally in the breadcrumbs, pressing to adhere.

MAKES 12 BUNS
75 g (2¾ oz/½ cup) plain (all-purpose) flour
2 eggs, beaten
160 g (5½ oz/2 cups) fresh breadcrumbs
12 buns for steaming (p.129)
125 ml (4 fl oz/½ cup) grapeseed oil
24 thin slices cucumber
¼ cup picked coriander (cilantro) leaves

PRESSED PIG'S HEAD
1 teaspoon ground Chinese five-spice
1 teaspoon salt
½ pig's head or 1 kg (2 lb 3 oz)
   piece pork belly
1 red Asian shallot, finely diced
2 spring onions (scallions),
   white part only, thinly sliced
2 tablespoons coriander (cilantro),
   chopped
1½ tablespoons lime juice
1 tablespoon fish sauce
2 tablespoons sriracha sauce
2 tablespoons sweet soy sauce

CHILLI TAMARIND DRESSING
1 fresh long red chilli
6 dried long red chillies,
   soaked and seeded
1 tablespoon grapeseed oil
6 red Asian shallots, thinly sliced
3 garlic cloves, thinly sliced
3 coriander (cilantro) roots,
   cleaned of all dirt and roughly chopped
3 scud or bird's eye chillies,
   roughly chopped
2 tablespoons tamarind purée
1½ tablespoons sugar
2 tablespoons fish sauce
1 tablespoon lime juice

PIG'S HEAD BAO WITH
CHILLI TAMARIND DRESSING (CONTINUED)

Prepare the buns, place them in a bamboo steamer basket lined
with baking paper and set aside.

Heat the grapeseed oil in a frying pan over medium–low heat.
Fry the crumbed pork until golden on all sides.

Bring some water in a saucepan large enough to fit the bamboo steamer
to the boil. While the pork is cooking, steam the buns for 4–5 minutes or
until soft in the centre.

To finish, open the buns and place ½ teaspoon of tamarind dressing
onto each one, followed by a piece of fried pork, 2 slices of cucumber,
½ teaspoon more of tamarind dressing and some coriander.

See photograph (p.131).

↑
Wrangling a suckling pig, pre-banquet.

There's been an explosion in the availability and variety of Asian vegetables at local markets in Australia in the last twenty years or so, which has happily coincided with changes to the way I like to cook and eat. Vegetables have always played an important part in my cooking, and so this recent availability has not just been timely but has also been satisfying and inspiring.

Vegetables are probably the best ways to express the seasons in cooking and that's one of the reasons I like eating them. But I can happily eat a vegetarian dinner, not just because of the ingredients, the flavours and the techniques that go into each dish, but because of how it makes me feel at the end of a meal — lighter, more energetic, more positive.

I'd now rather eat more vegetables than protein and we include a lot of vegetable dishes on the menu at Supernormal. They're dishes that I would eat more frequently and return to more often.

Obviously vegetable dishes can be just as interesting as dishes focused on meat or fish but, until recently, this has not necessarily been represented on restaurant menus, which is something we're trying to address at Supernormal.

The recipes here are for vegetable dishes rather than vegetarian because some of them contain some meat, but with the usual dish hierarchy flipped around. The meat plays a supporting role to the vegetable's main event here, more of a seasoning, another layer of complexity or a quiet background hum than the principal focus. These dishes are definitely not sides. They're designed to be stand-alone dishes or served as a central part of a larger banquet.

This is not a traditional kimchi. The flavours are taken from the kimchi process and applied to marinate fresh vegetables. I particularly enjoy the freshness and crunch that the vegetables retain through this process.

BEAN SPROUTS
I like to serve these bean sprouts alongside the Beef intercostals with Korean chilli dressing (p. 85). These bean sprouts are best when marinated for 1 hour before serving.

Bring a large saucepan of water to the boil and blanch the bean sprouts for 30 seconds. Refresh in iced water. When the bean sprouts have cooled, strain and squeeze the excess water out of them with your hands. Combine with the kimchi base, mixing well.

GREEN BEANS
A great side to a main meal or terrific on their own. We serve these beans in the restaurant with a roast rack of pork.

Bring a large saucepan of water to the boil and blanch the beans for 2 minutes. Refresh in iced water. Strain the beans then pat them dry with paper towel. Slice them lengthways into long thin strips. Mix well with the kimchi base. Serve immediately.

SHISO
I like to take the finished shiso leaves and wrap them in pieces of raw tuna. They are also great roughly chopped and served simply with steamed rice.

Bring a large saucepan of water to the boil and blanch the leaves for 30 seconds. Refresh in iced water then strain in a colander. Lay the leaves on paper towel and dry well.

Take 1 shiso leaf and brush it with the kimchi base. Place another leaf on top of the first and brush with some more kimchi base. Repeat this process until all the leaves have been coated. Leave the leaves to marinate for a few hours in the refrigerator before using. Serve immediately.

SERVES 4

BEAN SPROUTS
200 g (7 oz) bean sprouts
1 tablespoon Kimchi base (p.219)

GREEN BEANS
200 g (7 oz) long green beans
1 tablespoon Kimchi base (p.219)

SHISO
12 large shiso leaves
1 tablespoon Kimchi base (p.219)

Bring a large saucepan of water to the boil. Season with a good pinch of sea salt and blanch the peas for 1 minute. Taste the peas and, if they are tender, drain them — otherwise cook for another minute or two.

Heat the grapeseed oil in a large frying pan over medium–high heat. Add the XO sauce and fry for 1 minute before adding the peas. Cook for 2 minutes then add the mustard leaf, cooking until the leaves have wilted. Season with a squeeze of lemon juice and sea salt to taste.

SERVES 4

sea salt
310 g (11 oz/2 cups) fresh peas
1 tablespoon grapeseed oil
60 ml (2 fl oz/¼ cup) XO sauce (p.218)
2 bunches mustard leaf, trimmed
½ lemon

BROAD BEANS WITH
PRESERVED SNOW VEGETABLE

Heat 1 tablespoon of the oil in a large frying pan over medium–high heat. Sauté half the broad beans for 3 minutes, then transfer them to a bowl and mash them roughly with a fork.

Reduce the heat and gently cook the garlic in the remaining oil, then add the rest of the broad beans and cook for 3 minutes. Add the crushed broad beans, snow vegetable, spring onion and mustard leaf, cooking until the leaves are just wilted. Season with a squeeze of lemon juice and sea salt to taste then serve.

SERVES 4 (AS PART OF A LARGER MEAL)

2 tablespoons grapeseed oil

350 g (12½ oz) podded broad (fava) beans, blanched and peeled (from 500 g/1 lb 2 oz unshelled beans)

1 garlic clove, finely chopped

2 tablespoons finely chopped preserved snow vegetable (potherb mustard)

3 spring onions (scallions), white part only, thinly sliced

2 bunches mustard leaf, trimmed and washed

½ lemon

sea salt

CHARRED BROCCOLINI
WITH MUSTARD DRESSING

This lovely clean vegetable dish makes an excellent stand-alone warm salad or a great accompaniment to a main course.

To make the mustard dressing, in a medium bowl whisk together the egg yolk and mustard. Add the oil slowly, whisking constantly, until it emulsifies. Whisk in the sugar and salt followed by the soy sauce, vinegar and yuzu juice. Set aside.

Bring a medium saucepan of water to the boil.

Prepare the broccolini by trimming off the tough ends. Boil the broccolini for 2 minutes and then place in iced water to cool.

Preheat the oven to 160°C (320°F).

Warm 1 teaspoon of the grapeseed oil in a frying pan over medium heat. Add the panko breadcrumbs, stir until golden then remove from the heat and set aside.

Peel the boiled egg and press it through a sieve to create a crumb effect. Set aside.

Spread the bonito flakes on a baking tray lined with baking paper. Lightly toast the bonito flakes in the oven for 1–2 minutes.

Remove the broccolini from the water and pat dry with a tea (dish) towel. Toss the broccolini in a bowl with the remaining oil and a pinch of sea salt.

Heat a chargrill pan or barbecue until very hot. Place the broccolini on the grill and cook for 2 minutes each side or until nicely charred.

To finish, toss the broccolini with half the mustard dressing. Arrange on a serving plate, adding more dressing if desired. Sprinkle the egg over the broccolini, then the breadcrumbs and finally the toasted bonito flakes.

SERVES 4
3 bunches broccolini
2 tablespoons grapeseed oil
20 g (¾ oz/⅓ cup) panko breadcrumbs
1 egg, boiled for 10 minutes
2 tablespoons dried bonito flakes
sea salt

MUSTARD DRESSING
1 egg yolk
2 teaspoons Dijon mustard
60 ml (2 fl oz/¼ cup) grapeseed oil
1 teaspoon sugar
pinch of salt
1½ tablespoons light soy sauce
2 teaspoons rice wine vinegar
2 teaspoons yuzu juice

CHRYSANTHEMUM LEAF SALAD WITH
GINGER AND SESAME DRESSING

To make the ginger and sesame dressing, combine all the ingredients in a bowl and set aside.

Tear the iceberg lettuce into rough pieces. In a serving bowl, gently toss the chrysanthemum and iceberg leaves with 2 tablespoons of the dressing and a pinch of salt. Taste the salad and add more salt and dressing if required.

SERVES 4 (AS A SIDE SALAD)
¼ iceberg lettuce
½ cup chrysanthemum leaves
sea salt

GINGER AND SESAME DRESSING
1½ tablespoons ginger vinegar
1¼ tablespoons white sesame oil
2 tablespoons grapeseed oil
1 tablespoon rice vinegar

↑
Night moves.
←
Smoked eggplant, sesame, furikake (p.146).

SMOKED EGGPLANT, SESAME, FURIKAKE

The key here is to prepare a fire or grill to cook the eggplant. A wood fire gives a depth of flavour that pushes this dish to the next level.

To make the ponzu dressing, in a small saucepan over medium heat, bring the ponzu base, soy sauce and 1 tablespoon water to a simmer. Add the bonito and mix well. Remove from the heat and leave to infuse for 30 minutes. Pass through a fine sieve and discard the bonito.

To make the sesame dressing, in a small bowl, combine the tahini paste, soy sauce, sugar and salt. Whisk in about 60 ml (2 fl oz/¼ cup) water until the sauce is the consistency of thick but pourable cream. Add more water if needed. Set aside.

Preheat a barbecue or chargrill pan to high.

Poke a few holes in the skin of the eggplants with a metal skewer and grill the whole eggplants until nicely charred on the outside and tender inside, about 10–15 minutes.

Put the eggplants on a tray, cover with plastic wrap and leave to cool. Once cool, peel the skin off the eggplants and tear the flesh into strips (or leave whole if using small eggplants).

Put the cooked eggplant in a bowl and dress with 60 ml (2 fl oz/¼ cup) of the sesame dressing.

To serve, place 2 tablespoons of sesame dressing on a serving plate and arrange the eggplant on top. Dress the dish with 3 teaspoons of ponzu dressing and sprinkle generously with furikake.

See photograph (p.144).

SERVES 6

10 long Japanese eggplants (aubergines)
  or 6 small heirloom eggplants
Furikake (p.221) to serve

PONZU DRESSING
80 ml (2½ fl oz/⅓ cup) Ponzu base (p.219)
60 ml (2 fl oz/¼ cup) light soy sauce
10 g (¼ oz) shaved bonito

SESAME DRESSING
90 g (3 oz/⅓ cup) tahini paste
1 teaspoon light soy sauce
½ teaspoon sugar
¼ teaspoon salt

SILKEN TOFU, MARINATED EGGPLANT,
YUXIANG SAUCE

I like to use Yenson's brand tofu for this recipe. It's a cylinder-shaped
tofu with a fantastic texture that's made in Melbourne.

Peel the eggplants and place them in a steamer over a saucepan
of vigorously boiling water. Steam for about 15 minutes or until a
knife penetrates the flesh with no resistance. When the eggplants
are cooked, transfer them to a colander on a plate and leave in
the refrigerator to cool.

When cool, cut the eggplants into 1.5 cm (½ in) dice. Spoon the Yuxiang
sauce over the eggplant and leave to marinate for 15 minutes.

Meanwhile, slice the tofu into discs and arrange on a serving plate.
Spoon the eggplant over and around the tofu. Finish the dish with a
dash of chilli oil, the coriander and a sprinkling of the Sichuan pepper.

SERVES 4
2 eggplants (aubergines)
80 ml (2½ fl oz/⅓ cup)
   Yuxiang sauce (p.218)
250 g (9 oz) tube of silken tofu
1 tablespoon chilli oil
5 coriander (cilantro) sprigs
1 teaspoon Sichuan peppercorns,
   ground

BRUSSELS SPROUTS
AND CHINESE SAUSAGE

This is a great vegetable dish that we serve in winter at Supernormal. The sweetness of the lap cheong wins over most opponents of the brussels sprout. We always use the tiniest organic brussels sprouts available — they're less bitter and have a tighter, firmer texture.

In a bowl, whisk together all the ingredients for the dressing. Check the seasoning and set aside.

Trim the brussels sprouts of any loose outer leaves and cut them in half lengthways. Slice the sausage thinly, on an angle.

Heat the grapeseed oil in a frying pan over medium heat. Add the brussels sprouts, cut side down, and sauté until golden and caramelised, about 5 minutes — you may have to do this in batches if the sprouts don't all fit in your pan. Turn the sprouts over and repeat. Add the sausage and sauté for 3 minutes, tossing the contents of the pan regularly. Remove the pan from the heat and transfer the sprouts to a mixing bowl. Repeat the process until all the brussels sprouts are cooked.

Just before serving, add the dressing to the sprouts and mix well. Serve warm.

SERVES 4 (AS A SIDE DISH)
300 g (10½ oz) brussels sprouts
2 lap cheong (Chinese sausages)
2 tablespoons grapeseed oil

DRESSING
1½ tablespoons rice wine vinegar
1 tablespoon fish sauce
1 tablespoon mirin
2 teaspoons light soy sauce
1 tablespoon water
1 teaspoon lemon juice
1 small bird's eye chilli, finely chopped
2 teaspoons grapeseed oil
1 teaspoon sugar

GRILLED ASPARAGUS
WITH CHINESE SAUSAGE

To make the mayonnaise, bring a small saucepan of water to the boil, add the egg and cook for 5 minutes. Cool the egg in a bowl of iced water.

Peel the egg and put in a medium bowl then break it up into small pieces with a fork. Whisk in the mustard then whisk in the oil, little by little, until it is emulsified. Stir in the lemon juice and pickled mustard stem and season with salt and white pepper.

Gently warm 1 teaspoon of the grapeseed oil in a saucepan over medium heat. Add the sausage and cook for 5 minutes, stirring frequently. Set aside to cool. Once cool, use a mortar and pestle to pound the sausage until it resembles rough crumbs.

Trim the tough ends off the asparagus. Heat a chargrill pan or barbecue until very hot. Toss the asparagus in the remaining grapeseed oil and grill for 2 minutes on each side or until nicely charred.

Remove the asparagus from the grill, lightly season with sea salt and slice the spears into 3 on a sharp angle.

To serve, place a spoonful of mayonnaise on a serving plate and arrange the asparagus on top. Spoon more mayonnaise in and around the asparagus. Finish by sprinkling over the sausage crumb and lemon juice.

SERVES 4

2 teaspoons grapeseed oil
2 Chinese sausages (lap cheong), finely diced
2 bunches asparagus
sea salt
½ teaspoon lemon juice

MAYONNAISE

1 egg
½ teaspoon Dijon mustard
60 ml (2 fl oz/¼ cup) grapeseed oil
1 teaspoon lemon juice
2 teaspoons finely chopped pickled mustard stem
ground white pepper
sea salt

The baby corn we use here is available at markets in spring and is usually available all the way through to late summer. Cooked whole in the husk the flavour is contained and concentrated by the corn silk, the fine strands inside the husk. When the corn is this young, the silk is edible and full of flavour.

In a small bowl, whisk the butter and miso until well combined. Spoon the butter into a piping (icing) bag and set aside.

Steam the corn over rapidly boiling water for 4 minutes.

Heat a barbecue or chargrill pan until very hot. Grill the corn for 4–5 minutes, turning regularly until it is nicely charred all over. Set the corn aside to cool for 5 minutes.

With a sharp knife, cut a slit down the middle of one side of the husk without cutting into the corn, then carefully open the husk to reveal the cob. Pipe a small line of miso butter down the middle of each corn cob, sprinkle generously with shichimi togarashi and serve.

SERVES 6

80 g (2¾ oz) unsalted butter,
   at room temperature
2 tablespoons white miso paste
12 baby corn, husks on and
   tips trimmed
1 tablespoon shichimi togarashi
   (Japanese chilli powder)

SAUTÉED MUSHROOMS, CRISP RICE CAKES, SOY DRESSING

To make the rice cakes, in a large saucepan over medium heat, gently heat 25 ml (¾ fl oz) of the grapeseed oil. Add the ginger and cook for 3 minutes until soft and slightly caramelised. Add the mushrooms and cook for a further 3 minutes. Once sweated down, add the rice, stirring constantly for 5 minutes. Turn the heat to high add the remaining ingredients. Stir well and bring to the boil.

Transfer the rice to a 25 x 20 cm (10 x 8 in) roasting tray and spread it out evenly. Place the tray in a steamer (at approximately 100°C/210°F) and let it cook for 25–30 minutes. Remove the rice from the steamer and fluff it with a fork.

Transfer the rice to a similar sized tray lined with plastic wrap. Place another layer of plastic wrap on top and press the cake flat and even. It should be about 2 cm (¾ in) thick. Transfer to the refrigerator until the rice cake has set. Once set, portion the cake into 3 cm (1¼ in) squares.

In a small bowl, whisk the black vinegar, soy sauces and 1½ tablespoons grapeseed oil together until well combined.

Put the kohlrabi in a small saucepan, add the salt and pour in enough water to just cover. Bring to the boil and then turn heat to a simmer, cooking for about 20 minutes or until the kohlrabi offers no resistance to the tip of a sharp knife. Drain well, then mash and pass through a fine sieve. Check the seasoning and keep warm.

Gently warm 2 tablespoons of the grapeseed oil in a non-stick frying pan. Place 8 squares of rice cake into the pan and cook until nicely golden. Turn the cakes and repeat until golden on all sides.

Meanwhile heat the remaining grapeseed oil in another frying pan. Add the mushrooms and sauté for 4–5 minutes or until golden. Add the garlic chives and cook for a further minute. Remove the mushrooms from the heat and add 1 tablespoon of the dressing.

Place a generous amount of kohlrabi purée on a serving plate, followed by the rice cakes. Arrange the mushrooms over the top and drizzle with a little more of the dressing.

SERVES 6

1 tablespoon Chinese black vinegar
2 tablespoons light soy sauce
60 ml (2 fl oz/¼ cup) sweet soy sauce
1½ tablespoons grapeseed oil
1 kohlrabi, peeled and diced
½ teaspoon sea salt
2 cups mixed mushrooms such as shimeji, chestnut, oyster, king brown
80 ml (2½ fl oz/⅓ cup) grapeseed oil
2 tablespoons finely chopped garlic chives

RICE CAKES

60 ml (2 fl oz/¼ cup) grapeseed oil
20 g (¾oz) chopped fresh ginger
60 g (2 oz) chopped king brown mushrooms
500 g (1 lb 2 oz) glutinous (sticky) rice
650 ml (22 fl oz) water
75 ml (2½ fl oz) soy sauce
¼ teaspoon salt
25 ml (¾ fl oz) Chinese black vinegar
50 ml (1¾ fl oz) light soy sauce
70 ml (2¼ fl oz) sweet soy sauce

↑
The energy of the open kitchen.

Yuzu kosho is a fermented paste made from ground yuzu citrus peel and green chillies.

To make the yuzu kosho dressing, whisk all the ingredients together in a small bowl. Set aside.

Assess your tomatoes — if the larger tomatoes have thick skin, remove it by plunging the tomatoes into a saucepan of boiling water for 15 seconds. Immediately transfer them to a bowl of iced water to cool, then peel the skin off with a small knife.

Cut the larger tomatoes into 1 cm (½ in) thick slices or wedges and place them in a bowl. Smaller tomatoes can simply be halved or quartered.

Add the shallot and shiso to the tomatoes and season with a little sea salt. Gently toss 60 ml (2 fl oz/¼ cup) of the dressing through the tomatoes. Taste one of the tomatoes and add a touch more dressing if necessary.

Slice the tofu into 1 cm (½ in) thick discs and arrange them on a serving plate. Place the tomatoes on and around the tofu. Drizzle over a little more dressing and finish with the fried shallots and torn basil leaves.

SERVES 4

500 g (1 lb 2 oz) assorted, perfectly ripe heirloom tomatoes
1 large red Asian shallot, thinly sliced
1 teaspoon finely chopped shiso leaf (about 3 leaves)
sea salt
125 g (4½ oz) tube of silken tofu
2 tablespoons Fried shallots (p.221) to serve
torn basil leaves to serve

YUZU KOSHO DRESSING
20 ml (¾ fl oz) rice wine vinegar
20 ml (¾ fl oz) soy sauce
10 ml (¼ fl oz) ginger vinegar
20 ml (¾ fl oz) grapeseed oil
5 g (¼ oz) yuzu kosho paste

This is the only recipe at Supernormal that travelled with us from Golden Fields. It's one of the most popular dishes we make and we've kept making it because I suspect there might be a riot if we tried to take it off the menu. There's something about the way the Kewpie mayonnaise and the bun get together that just seems to hit a particular bliss spot. Local lobster, freshly cooked is really the only way to go here. If you don't want to cook the lobster yourself, you can get it from your fishmonger — just check ahead so that you can be sure it has been freshly cooked.

↑
Lobster, pre-roll.
←
A perfectly formed fridge-magnet hand roll.

Bring a large saucepan of water to the boil over high heat, then reduce the heat to medium until the water is at a constant simmer.

Poach the lobster tail in its shell in the simmering water for about 8–10 minutes. Remove the lobster from the pan and set aside to cool. Place in the refrigerator until chilled.

Shell the lobster and slice the meat into 8 discs. Finely chop any small or discoloured pieces of lobster you may have.

Cut the shallot in half lengthways and thinly slice each half.

Pick the watercress, discarding any bruised or tarnished leaves, then wash and pat dry.

Combine the Kewpie mayonnaise, lemon juice, vinegar and mustard powder in a mixing bowl. Slowly add the oil while whisking continuously. Season to taste.

Preheat the oven to 180°C (350°F).

Cut the brioche buns in half horizontally and lightly butter them. Put the buns on a tray, butter side down, and toast them in the oven for 5 minutes or until golden brown.

Spread 1 teaspoon of the mayonnaise onto each half of the brioche. Place a tablespoon of chopped lobster on the bottom halves and season to taste. Arrange 2 discs of lobster meat on top without overlapping. Place ½ teaspoon mayonnaise on each lobster slice and season again to taste. Add a few slices of shallot and a few leaves of watercress, place the brioche lid on the top and serve immediately.

MAKES 4 ROLLS

1 lobster tail in its shell
1 red Asian shallot
½ bunch watercress
125 g (4½ oz/½ cup) Kewpie mayonnaise
2 teaspoons lemon juice
1 teaspoon white wine vinegar
1 teaspoon mustard powder
60 ml (2 fl oz/¼ cup) olive oil
4 brioche buns
40 g (1½ oz) butter, softened

↑
Lobster rolls in full swing.
→
#goodfoodcrapdrawing.

What I enjoy about the dishes in this chapter is that they celebrate the shared table. They can all be served as part of a main meal and are best delivered to the centre of the table in a pan or on a serving plate. Of course they can also be eaten as stand-alone dishes but they've been designed with sharing in mind.

When I create a meal I usually start with the main dish protein that I've decided to serve and that in turn impacts and informs what I'll be serving with it, around it and before it. For example, if I'm serving a whole fish, I might start with an offal (variety meat) plate and some pickles, so there isn't fish all the way through the meal. It's about creating balance, thinking about how each element works with the others — starting with the central dish and working back from there.

With protein-based dishes I like to cook as much of the protein on the bone as possible — say a half duck, or a lamb shoulder or a whole fish. Cooking this way helps impart the flavour and retain moisture. It's a style that secondary cuts, like short ribs, respond to really well.

The dishes in this chapter have influences that are very much grounded in China and Japan, but there are European and modern Australian influences here as well. There are some classic European techniques, which have been altered slightly just by bringing in other flavours like miso and soy sauce which, when used correctly, can add another dimension to a dish without killing it and turning it into a heavy-handed fusion bomb. It's all about understanding and respecting the origins of a dish.

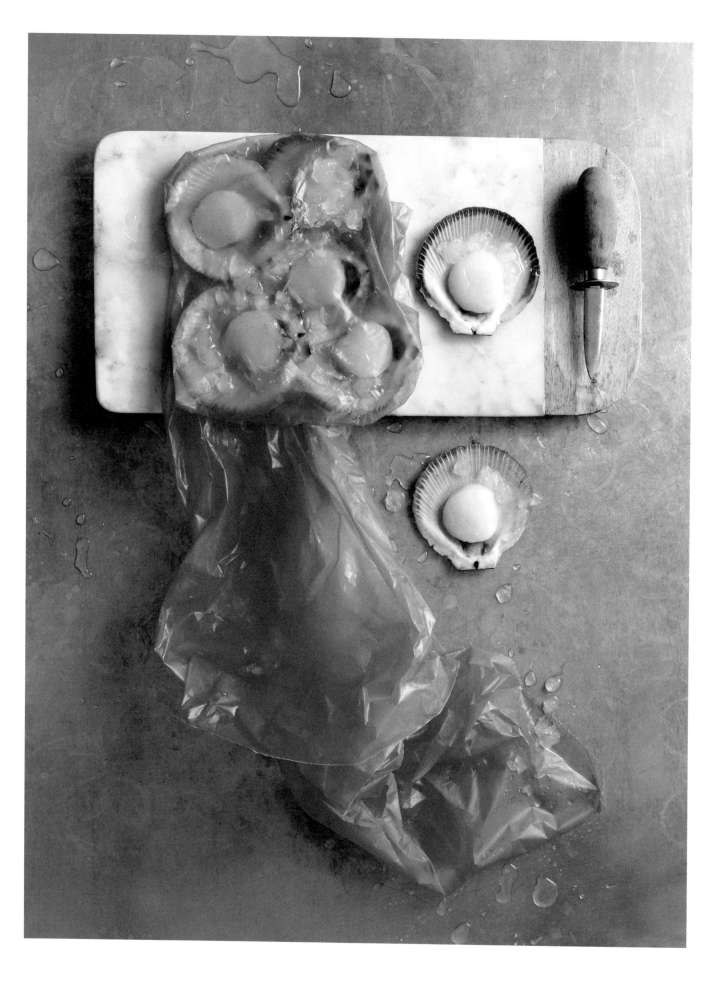

STEAMED HAPUKA, PRAWNS, DRIED SCALLOP SAUCE

Hapuka is a wonderful fish to steam or add to a seafood stew. If unavailable, grouper is a good substitute for this dish.

To make the dried scallop sauce, wipe the kombu with a damp cloth to clean it. Put it in a saucepan with the room temperature water and heat to 60°C (140°F) — when you start seeing steam. Remove the pan from the heat and leave it to steep for 1 hour, then remove and discard the kombu.

Meanwhile, soak the dried scallops in the warm water until they are plump. Drain the scallops and reserve the soaking water. Tear the scallops into fine shreds.

In a large saucepan, bring the kombu water, shredded scallops and 60 ml (2 fl oz/¼ cup) of the scallop soaking water to a simmer.

Mix the cornflour with 1 tablespoon water in a small bowl. Whisk the slurry into the simmering scallop water and let it cook for 2 minutes, stirring constantly. Remove from the heat and season the sauce with the soy sauce and vinegar. Taste for seasoning and set aside.

Bring a large saucepan of water to the boil. Plunge the spinach into the water, blanch for 30 seconds, strain and place the spinach in a bowl of iced water. Transfer the cooled spinach to a colander and squeeze as much water out of it as you can, then roughly chop and set it aside.

Steam the hapuka for 4–5 minutes or until just cooked.

While the fish is steaming, put the dried scallop sauce and shiitake mushrooms in a saucepan and bring to a simmer over medium heat. Add the prawns and cook for 2 minutes. Add the spinach and spring onion and stir to combine. Season with lemon juice and sea salt to taste.

Transfer the fish to 6 warm shallow bowls. Ladle the spinach, prawns and broth over each piece of fish and serve.

SERVES 6

400 g (14 oz) baby English spinach
6 x 130 g (4½ oz) pieces hapuka,
  skinned and trimmed
80 g (2¾ oz) fresh shiitake mushrooms,
  diced
12 raw prawns (shrimp),
  cleaned and sliced in half lengthways
2 spring onions (scallions),
  white part only, thinly sliced
juice of ½ lemon
sea salt

DRIED SCALLOP SAUCE

5 g (¼ oz) kombu
250 ml (8½ fl oz/1 cup) water,
  at room temperature
100 ml (3½ fl oz) warm water
20 g (¾ oz) dried scallops
1 tablespoon cornflour (cornstarch)
3 tablespoons light soy sauce
3 teaspoons sweet ginger vinegar

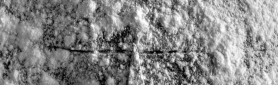

WHOLE ROASTED FISH, SWEET GINGER DRESSING, SEAWEED BUTTER

The seaweed paste we use in this recipe can be found in Asian grocery stores. It's called shimanoka iwa nori, it also comes under the English name of laver or laverbread.

To make the seaweed butter, take a large bowl and fill it with cold water. Crush the nori into small pieces, add it to the water and leave to soften for 10 minutes. Strain the nori (discarding the liquid) and squeeze out the excess water. Chop the nori into a rough paste.

In a medium bowl, combine the nori, butter, seaweed paste and lemon juice. Beat together until well combined then set aside.

Using a mandoline with a julienne attachment, slice the potato into thin slivers. Place the slivers in a bowl of cold water. Rinse the potato 2–3 times, in fresh water each time, to remove all the starch. Drain the potato and spread it out on a clean tea (dish) towel to dry thoroughly.

Place 2 tablespoons of the grapeseed oil in a large, non-stick frying pan or wok over high heat. Stir-fry the potato until it is cooked but still retains a little crispness, about 4–5 minutes. Remove the potato from the pan and season with 2 tablespoons of the sweet ginger dressing.

Preheat the oven to 180°C (350°F).

If your flounder is very large, cut its head off so the fish will fit neatly in a large ovenproof frying pan.

With a pair of kitchen scissors, trim the fins and tail, then rinse the fish and pat it dry.

Lay the flounder on a chopping board and score it by cutting 1 cm (½ in) deep slits evenly across the top of the fish. Season the fish with sea salt.

Add the remainder of the grapeseed oil to the frying pan and place it over high heat. Put the flounder in the hot pan, scored side down, and cook for about 2 minutes until the skin is golden and crispy. Using a spatula, carefully turn the fish over and transfer the pan to the oven to cook for 3–4 minutes. Remove the pan from the oven and check that the fish is cooked — the flesh exposed by the cuts should be opaque, not translucent. When the flounder is cooked, transfer it to a warm serving platter.

Quickly tip out any excess oil from the pan the fish was cooked in, and place the pan over low heat. Add the seaweed butter and stir it as it melts, until you have a thick emulsion. Pour the seaweed butter over the fish, completely covering it. Top with the potato and spring onion. Drizzle the completed dish with the remaining sweet ginger dressing.

SERVES 4-6

1 large desiree or other waxy potato, peeled
80 ml (2½ fl oz/⅓ cup) grapeseed oil
60 ml (2 fl oz/¼ cup) Sweet ginger dressing (p.219)
1 whole flounder (about 600–700 g/1 lb 5 oz–1 lb 9 oz)
sea salt
2 spring onions (scallions), green tops only, thinly sliced diagonally

SEAWEED BUTTER

2 sheets nori
50 g (1¾ oz) butter, softened
1½ teaspoons seaweed paste (shimanoka iwa nori)
¼ teaspoon lemon juice

STEAMED JOHN DORY, DAIKON, MUSSELS, CRUSTACEAN SAUCE

The crustacean sauce here is based on a classic that's been adapted. I've also used the base of this dish for a larger one-pot, slow-cooked seafood stew with great results.

To make the crustacean sauce, in a saucepan over high heat, sauté the onion, celery and carrot in the grapeseed oil until golden.

Meanwhile roughly chop the crab and crayfish head, removing the head gills from both. Add them to the pan and cook until aromatic, stirring constantly. Add the brandy and deglaze the pan until the liquid is reduced by half. Add the sake and reduce by half again.

Add the stock, 375 ml (12½ fl oz/1½ cups) water, the tomatoes, kombu and Korean chilli paste and cook gently for 45 minutes. Top up with water if the stock reduces too much. Add the miso paste and continue to cook for a further 15 minutes. Turn off the heat and leave the stock to cool slightly for 15 minutes. Taste and adjust the seasoning with a little light soy sauce if needed.

In a small saucepan, bring 250 ml (8½ fl oz/1 cup) of the crustacean sauce and 250 ml (8½ fl oz/1 cup) water to a simmer. Add the daikon and cook for 20 minutes or until tender.

Blanch the spring onions in boiling water for 30 seconds and refresh in iced water. Drain on paper towel and squeeze out the excess water. Finely chop the spring onions and then mix with the chilli oil in a bowl.

Steam the mussels and fish for 3–4 minutes or until barely cooked.

While the fish is cooking, reheat the remaining crustacean sauce until hot. Season the fish with a squeeze of lemon juice.

To serve, place the daikon in four individual serving bowls and place the steamed John Dory on top. Remove the mussels from the shells, pinch out their 'beards' and place the mussels on and around the fish. Pour 60 ml (2 fl oz/¼ cup) of the sauce around the fish and finish with a generous sprinkling of the spring onion.

SERVES 4

1 small daikon (white radish),
    peeled and cut into 1 cm (½ in) rounds
8 spring onions (scallions),
    white part only, washed and trimmed
1 teaspoon chilli oil
12 mussels
4 x 130 g (4½ oz) pieces of John Dory,
    or other white-fleshed fish,
    skinned and trimmed
½ lemon

CRUSTACEAN SAUCE

¼ onion, diced
½ celery stalk, diced
½ carrot, diced
2 tablespoons grapeseed oil
1 blue swimmer crab or mud crab
1 crayfish head (available from your
    fishmonger) or 1 cup prawn
    (shrimp) heads
60 ml (2 fl oz/¼ cup) brandy
250 ml (8½ fl oz/1 cup) cooking sake
500 ml (17 fl oz/2 cups) chicken stock
250 g (9 oz) peeled tomatoes
5 cm (2 in) piece kombu, washed
30 g (1 oz) Korean chilli paste
30 g (1 oz) white miso paste
light soy sauce for seasoning

FRIED CHICKEN WITH STICKY SAUCE

I prefer to use chicken legs for fried chicken, because the flavour and moisture content is superior to skinless boneless thighs. Our concoction of different flours ensures a crisp crust, which holds up beautifully to the sticky sauce.

To make the sticky sauce, in a stainless steel saucepan over medium heat, gently warm the grapeseed oil. Add the ginger and garlic and cook for 3–4 minutes until aromatic and wilted. Pour in the Shaoxing rice wine and cook until reduced by half. Add the glucose, soy sauce, chilli and spring onion and cook for 5–10 minutes until the sauce resembles a thick syrup. Remove the pan from the heat and stir through the rice wine vinegar. Set aside.

Season the chicken with a generous pinch of salt and place it in a single layer on a plate in the refrigerator for 2 hours.

Pat the chicken dry, put it in a bowl and pour over the buttermilk, stirring to coat the chicken.

Meanwhile, put the vegetable oil in a large, deep, heavy-based saucepan and heat it to 170°C (340°F).

While the oil is heating, mix all the flours together in a large bowl.

Remove the chicken pieces from the buttermilk and toss them through the flour until well coated.

Fry the chicken in 2 batches for 10–12 minutes each, or until the skin is golden and crisp. Remove the chicken from the oil and transfer to paper towel to drain.

When all the chicken is cooked, place it in a large bowl with the coriander sprigs, if using, and drizzle over 80 ml (2½ fl oz/⅓ cup) of the sticky sauce. Gently mix the chicken through the sauce until well coated. Taste and add more sticky sauce if necessary and serve.

SERVES 2-4

4 chicken leg quarters (marylands),
   each cut into 4 pieces
   (ask your butcher to do this)
sea salt
125 ml (4 fl oz/½ cup) buttermilk
2 litres (68 fl oz/8 cups) vegetable oil
   for deep-frying
90 g (3 oz/½ cup) rice flour
70 g (2½ oz/½ cup) tapioca flour
90 g (3 oz/½ cup) glutinous
   (sticky) rice flour
5 coriander (cilantro) sprigs, picked,
   for garnish (optional)

STICKY SAUCE

2 tablespoons grapeseed oil
1.5 cm (½ in) piece fresh ginger,
   finely chopped
8 garlic cloves, finely chopped
2 tablespoons Shaoxing rice wine
115 g (4 oz/⅓ cup) liquid glucose
80 ml (2½ fl oz/⅓ cup) light soy sauce
½ long red chilli, thinly sliced
1 spring onion (scallion),
   white part only, thinly sliced
2 tablespoons rice wine vinegar

↑
All systems go in the Supernormal kitchen.

TWICE-COOKED DUCK LEGS, PLUM SAUCE, STEAMED BREAD

An interactive dish that requires some pre-thought but is easy at the serving end of the process because your guests finish the preparation by constructing their own bao.

To make the duck legs, in a large bowl combine the Sichuan pepper, five-spice, sea salt flakes, ginger and spring onion, mixing well. Massage this curing mix into the duck legs and refrigerate the duck in a covered container for 12 hours, to cure. Once cured, wash the curing mix off the duck under cold water. Steam the duck legs over boiling water for 3 hours, topping the pan up with extra water as necessary. Once cooked, place the duck legs on a tray lined with baking paper and refrigerate them overnight, leaving the legs uncovered so they can dry out.

To make the steamed bread, combine the bread mix and sugar in a bowl. Slowly add the milk and oil, mixing well to form a dough. Knead the dough on a work surface for 3–4 minutes until it forms a smooth ball. Divide the dough into 30 g (1 oz) portions and roll each piece into a ball. Cover and leave to rest for 30 minutes. Dust a work surface with a little flour and roll out a piece of dough into an oval shape. Brush the piece of dough with oil and fold it over to make a half-moon shaped bread pocket. Place it on a small square piece of greaseproof (waxed) paper and place in the refrigerator. When all the pieces of dough have been rolled and folded they can be left in the refrigerator until you're ready to cook them.

Bring a large saucepan of water fitted with a steamer to the boil. Place the buns in the steamer in a single layer on greaseproof paper and steam over rapidly boiling water for 15 minutes.

Fill a large, heavy-based saucepan one-third full with oil and heat it to 190°C (375°F).

In a small bowl, combine the soy sauce with the yellow bean paste. Brush the mixture over the cooked duck legs then dust them lightly with flour.

Deep-fry the duck legs for 4–5 minutes until dark golden, then drain on paper towel.

To make the vinegar sauce, in a small bowl combine all the ingredients.

To serve, place the steamed bread on a platter, arrange the duck legs and cucumber rounds on another platter and serve with both the plum and vinegar sauces in small bowls on the side. At the table, shred the meat from the bone and make up little buns with plum sauce, cucumber and the duck meat. Dip the stuffed buns in the vinegar sauce just before you eat them.

See photograph (p.178).

SERVES 6

vegetable oil for deep-frying
2 tablespoons light soy sauce
2 tablespoons yellow bean paste
plain (all-purpose) flour for dusting
1 cucumber, peeled and sliced
 into 5 mm (¼ in) rounds
Plum sauce (p.218)

DUCK LEGS

1 teaspoon ground Sichuan pepper
1 teaspoon Chinese five-spice
2 tablespoons sea salt flakes
1.5 cm (½ in) piece fresh ginger, grated
2 spring onions (scallions),
 white part only, thinly sliced
6 duck legs

VINEGAR SAUCE

2.5 cm (1 in) piece fresh ginger, grated
2 tablespoons finely chopped coriander
 (cilantro) root
2 tablespoons kecap manis
2 tablespoons light soy sauce
2 tablespoons Chinese black vinegar
2 tablespoons water

STEAMED BREAD

450 g (1 lb) Rooster brand
 steamed bun cake flour
55 g (2 oz/¼ cup) caster
 (superfine) sugar
250 ml (8½ fl oz/1 cup) milk
1 teaspoon grapeseed oil,
 plus extra for greasing
plain (all-purpose) flour for dusting

↑
Interactive: duck bao.
←
Twice-cooked duck legs, plum sauce, steamed bread (p.177).

ROAST PORK SHOULDER, PICKLED CABBAGE, CRACKLING, SSAMJANG

This roast pork dish is epic. Complete with crackling, steamed bread and an arrangement of pickles and vegetables, it's a complete banquet worthy of any celebration.

To make the ssamjang, mix all the ingredients together and set aside.

To make the steamed bread, in a bowl combine the flour and sugar. Using your hand, mix the flour and sugar while slowly adding the milk and oil to form a dough. Knead the dough on a work surface for 3–4 minutes until it forms a smooth ball.

Divide the dough into 10 equal pieces and roll each piece into a ball. Place on a tray and leave to rest in the refrigerator for 30 minutes.

When you are ready to serve the bread, steam the dough balls over rapidly boiling water until the bread rises, about 12–15 minutes.

With a sharp knife, score the pork skin, or you can ask your butcher to do this for you.

Place a steamer — large enough to fit the pork — on the stove and bring it to a simmer. Place the pork shoulder in the steamer and cook it for 4 hours.

Preheat the oven to 200°C (400°F).

Remove the pork from the steamer and place it in a large, heavy roasting tin. Rub the oil over the pork skin and sprinkle with the salt. Roast in the oven for 30–45 minutes or until the skin is crisp.

Serve the pork with the steamed bread, pickled cabbage, ssamjang and lemon cheeks.

SERVES 10

4 kg (8 lb 13 oz) pork shoulder, bone in and skin on
2 tablespoons grapeseed oil
2 teaspoons salt
Pickled cabbage (p.220)
4 lemons, cut into cheeks

SSAMJANG

60 g (2 oz/¼ cup) red chilli paste
60 g (2 oz/¼ cup) white miso paste
2 tablespoons rice wine vinegar
2 tablespoons honey
½ red onion, finely diced
2 garlic cloves, finely grated
thumb-sized piece fresh ginger, finely grated
2 spring onions (scallions), white part only, thinly sliced
2 long red chillies, finely diced

STEAMED BREAD

450 g (1 lb) Rooster brand steamed bun cake flour
115 g (4 oz/½ cup) caster (superfine) sugar
250 ml (8½ fl oz/1 cup) milk
1 teaspoon grapeseed oil

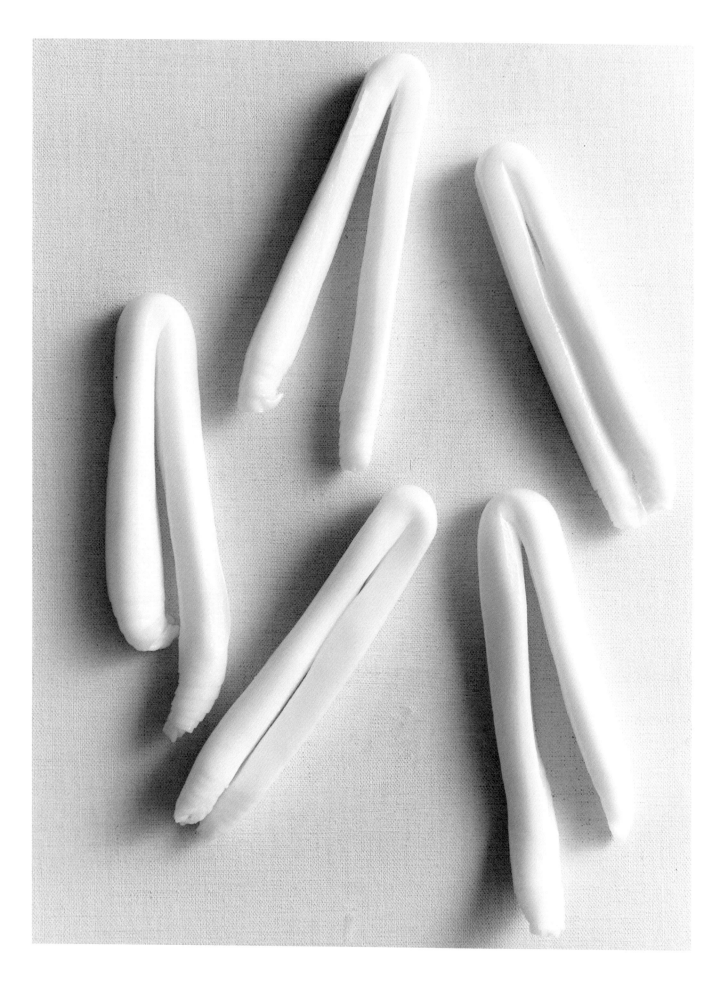

SPICY MINCED PORK, EGGPLANT, RICE NOODLES, SICHUAN SAUCE

To make the Sichuan sauce, heat the grapeseed oil in a large stainless steel saucepan. Add the shallot, garlic, ginger, spring onion and chilli and cook over medium heat for 3–4 minutes until aromatic and wilted. Add the chilli bean paste and the ground Sichuan peppercorns and cook for a further 2 minutes. Deglaze the pan with the Shaoxing rice wine and reduce by half. Add the tomatoes, soy sauce, vinegar, 250 ml (8½ fl oz/1 cup) water and the sugar. Bring to a simmer and cook for 15 minutes. Remove from the heat and season to taste with sea salt.

Heat 2 tablespoons of the grapeseed oil in a frying pan over medium–high heat and fry the pork mince until it is cooked through. Transfer the pork to a large saucepan and add 375 ml (12½ fl oz/1½ cups) of the Sichuan sauce and the chicken stock. Bring to a simmer and cook for 15–20 minutes until the sauce has reduced a little. Add water if the sauce is becoming too thick.

Meanwhile, slice the eggplant lengthways into 2 cm (¾ in) thick slices, then cut the slices lengthways into 2 cm (¾ in) wide strips. Cut these into 5 cm (2 in) lengths.

Heat the remaining grapeseed oil in a frying pan over medium heat. Sauté the eggplant pieces in batches until golden. Transfer to paper towel to drain.

Cut the rice noodles into 3 cm (1¼ in) lengths. Place the noodles on greaseproof (waxed) paper and transfer them to a steamer set over a pan of simmering water. Steam for 3 minutes or until the noodles are soft.

While the noodles are cooking, warm the eggplant in the minced pork sauce. When the noodles are ready add them to the Sichuan pork sauce and bring it back to a simmer.

Transfer the finished noodles and eggplant to a deep dish and drizzle with the chilli oil, sprinkle with the ground Sichuan pepper and top with the coriander sprigs.

SERVES 4

125 ml (4 fl oz/½ cup) grapeseed oil
250 g (9 oz) minced (ground) pork
125 ml (4 fl oz/½ cup) chicken stock or water
1 large eggplant (aubergine)
250 g (9 oz) rolled rice noodles (banh cuon)
1 tablespoon chilli oil
½ teaspoon Sichuan peppercorns, toasted and ground
½ bunch coriander (cilantro), sprigs picked, to serve

SICHUAN SAUCE

2 tablespoons grapeseed oil
1 red Asian shallot, finely diced
2 garlic cloves, finely chopped
1 tablespoon finely chopped ginger
2 spring onions (scallions), thinly sliced
2 long red chillies, seeded and thinly sliced
1 tablespoon fermented chilli bean paste
1 teaspoon Sichuan peppercorns, ground
1 tablespoon Shaoxing rice wine
100 g (3½ oz) tinned diced tomatoes
1 tablespoon light soy sauce
1 tablespoon Chinese black vinegar
1 teaspoon sugar
sea salt to taste

RIB EYE WITH BLACK PEPPER SAUCE

This dish takes the Australian pub staple of steak with pepper sauce and gives it a bit of a shake-up.

Remove the meat from the refrigerator 1 hour before you intend to cook it. Season the beef with plenty of salt.

Preheat a barbecue or chargrill pan until hot. Brush the meat with the grapeseed oil and place it on the hot grill. Cook to your preferred degree of doneness.

When the beef is cooked, remove it from the heat and set it aside in a warm place, loosely tented with foil, and allow it to rest for 15 minutes.

Just before carving your meat, reheat the black pepper sauce in a small saucepan and serve it with the meat.

SERVES 6

1 kg (2 lb 3 oz) beef rib eye or
    preferred cut of beef
sea salt
2 tablespoons grapeseed oil
Black pepper sauce (p.218)

BRAISED BEEF CHEEK, CRISP TRIPE, KATSUOBUSHI BUTTER

Trim the beef of any excess fat and sinew. Place it in a deep ovenproof dish or baking tin just wide enough to hold the beef in a single layer. Mix the sweet soy sauce and five-spice together and rub this mixture over the beef. Leave to marinate in the refrigerator for 3 hours or overnight.

To make the tripe, soak it in water overnight. The following day drain the tripe and place it in a saucepan of fresh water over medium heat. Bring the tripe to a simmer and cook for 15 minutes. Strain, discarding the water. Cover the tripe with fresh water and return it to the stove. Add the onion and cloves and bring back to a simmer. When cooked, remove the pan from the heat and leave to cool to room temperature. Strain the tripe and pat dry. Discard the onion and cloves.

Preheat the oven to 160°C (320°F).

To crisp the tripe, shred it into fine threads. Lay the tripe threads on a tray lined with a piece of baking paper and drizzle with the grapeseed oil. Cover with another piece of baking paper and top this with another tray to compress the tripe as it cooks. Bake for 30 minutes, checking it occasionally. As the tripe cooks it will become crisp and turn golden. When cooked, remove it from the oven and leave to cool and set. Slide it off the baking paper onto paper towel.

Reduce the oven temperature to 150°C (300°F).

To cook the beef, fill the dish with enough chicken stock to just cover the beef. Cover the dish with foil and cook in the oven for 3–4 hours or until the meat is tender but not falling apart. Top up with water as it cooks, if necessary. When tender, remove the dish from the oven and leave the meat to cool in its liquid in the refrigerator.

To make the katsuobushi butter, put the bonito flakes in a small bowl and pour over the boiling water. Allow to infuse for 20 minutes then strain and discard the bonito.

Transfer the liquid to a small saucepan over medium heat and reduce until you have 1 teaspoon of liquid.

Put the butter in a bowl and mix it with the bonito liquid and bonito flake powder. Season with a pinch of salt and a squeeze of lemon juice.

Increase the oven temperature to 180°C (350°F).

Prick the eggplants with a fork and place them in a baking dish. Bake for 30 minutes or until tender. Leave to cool.

Once cool, cut the eggplants in half and scoop out the flesh.

SERVES 4
800 g (1 lb 12 oz) beef cheeks
60 ml (2 fl oz/¼ cup) sweet soy sauce
1 teaspoon Chinese five-spice
500 ml (17 fl oz/2 cups) chicken stock
2 large eggplants (aubergines)
2 teaspoons light soy sauce
½ teaspoon sesame oil
2 tablespoons grapeseed oil
½ teaspoon rice wine vinegar
1 bunch mustard greens, trimmed

TRIPE
1 large piece honeycomb tripe
½ onion
3 cloves
1 tablespoon grapeseed oil

KATSUOBUSHI BUTTER
5 g (¼ oz) bonito flakes
2 tablespoons boiling water
60 g (2 oz) butter, softened
½ teaspoon bonito flake powder
sea salt
½ lemon

Place the flesh in an upright blender along with the light soy sauce and sesame oil. Blend until smooth and then slowly pour in the grapeseed oil and season with the vinegar. Set aside.

Put the cooked beef cheek in a saucepan with the cooking liquor and bring to a simmer over medium heat.

Melt 1 tablespoon of the katsuobushi butter in a large frying pan over medium heat. Add the mustard greens and cook until they are wilted. Remove the pan from the heat and finish with 1 more tablespoon of katsuobushi butter.

Heat up the eggplant purée in a small saucepan over medium heat until it is hot. Place the purée on serving plates and arrange the mustard greens around it. Cut the beef cheeks in half and place them on the plates. Top the beef with the crisp tripe and serve.

See photograph (p.189).

↑
Katsuobushi butter.
→
Braised beef cheek, crisp tripe,
katsuobushi butter (p.186).

WHOLE ROAST LAMB SHOULDER, CORIANDER
AND MINT PASTE, SICHUAN SAUCE

To make the Sichuan sauce, In a large stainless steel saucepan, warm the grapeseed oil over medium heat. Add the garlic and ginger, cooking for 3–4 minutes until aromatic. Add the chilli bean paste and cook for 2 minutes. Deglaze the pan with the Shaoxing rice wine and reduce by half. Add the tomatoes, sugar, yellow bean paste, oyster sauce and stock and bring to the boil. Reduce the heat and simmer for 30 minutes.

Combine the cornflour and vinegar with 1 tablespoon water and pour it into the sauce, stirring regularly as it thickens. Blend the sauce until it is smooth (a hand-held blender is best for this).

In a bowl, mix together the light soy sauce, yellow bean paste, Shaoxing rice wine, cumin, chilli flakes, five-spice and sugar.

Take a heavy, deep roasting tin large enough to fit the lamb shoulder. Rub the marinade all over the meat, put it in the tin, cover with plastic wrap and leave to marinate for a few hours or ideally overnight in the refrigerator.

Preheat the oven to 150°C (300°F).

Remove the plastic wrap from the lamb and add 250 ml (8½ fl oz/1 cup) water to the roasting tin. Cover the lamb tightly with aluminium foil and roast the lamb in the oven for 2 hours. Reduce the oven temperature to 110°C (230°F) and cook for a further 4 hours, checking every so often and adding a little more water if the tin becomes dry. Remove the foil for the last hour of roasting to crisp up the skin.

To make the coriander and mint paste, put the avocado, garlic, cumin, coriander and mint in an upright blender. Blend until you have a rough purée. Pour the oil in slowly, blending until the sauce becomes smooth. Season the sauce with the lemon juice and sea salt, adding more if necessary. Set aside.

When ready to serve, heat the grapeseed oil in a large non-stick frying pan over medium heat. Cook the spring onion pancakes for 2 minutes on each side or until golden.

Warm the Sichuan sauce over low heat.

Place the lamb in a deep dish and pour the Sichuan sauce over the top. Finish the dish with the chilli oil, ground Sichuan pepper, coriander and spring onion. Serve with the spring onion pancakes and the coriander and mint paste on the side.

SERVES 4

2 tablespoons light soy sauce
2 tablespoons yellow bean paste
2 tablespoons Shaoxing rice wine
1 tablespoon cumin seeds
1 tablespoon Korean chilli flakes
½ teaspoon Chinese five-spice
½ teaspoon sugar
1 x 1.5 kg (3 lb 5 oz) lamb shoulder, on the bone (you can also use lamb shanks or sliced neck on the bone)
2 tablespoons grapeseed oil
8 store-bought spring onion (scallion) pancakes
1 tablespoon chilli oil
½ teaspoon toasted and ground Sichuan peppercorns
small handful of coriander (cilantro) to serve
2 shredded spring onions (scallions) to serve

SICHUAN SAUCE

60 ml (2 fl oz/¼ cup) grapeseed oil
4 garlic cloves, finely chopped
2 tablespoons finely chopped fresh ginger
½ cup fermented chilli bean paste
2 tablespoons Shaoxing rice wine
225 g (8 oz) tin chopped tomatoes
3 tablespoons yellow rock sugar
3 tablespoons yellow bean paste
80 ml (2½ fl oz/⅓ cup) oyster sauce
1 litre (34 fl oz/4 cups) chicken stock or water
1 tablespoon cornflour (cornstarch)
1 tablespoon rice wine vinegar

CORIANDER AND MINT PASTE

½ avocado
1 garlic clove, roughly chopped
½ teaspoon cumin seeds, toasted
½ bunch coriander (cilantro), washed
½ cup loosely packed mint leaves
1½ tablespoons grapeseed oil
½ teaspoon lemon juice
½ teaspoon sea salt flakes

マンゴー 生クリーム
Mango fresh cream
¥410

ジェラート マンゴー生クリーム
Gelato Mango fresh cream
¥460

もOK!!

キャラメルアップル チーズケーキクリーム
CARAMEL APPLE
CHEESE CAKE & CREAM
¥500

ジェラート ベリーベリークリーム
GELATO BERRY BERRY
& CREAM
¥550

ダブルチョコ カスタードクリーム
DOUBLE CHOCOLATE
CUSTARD & CREAM
¥510

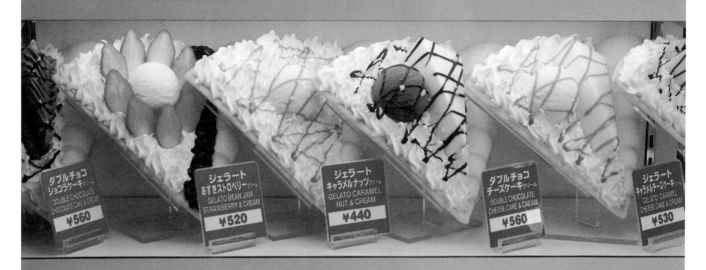

ダブルチョコ ショコラケーキクリーム
DOUBLE CHOCOLATE
CHOCOLATE CAKE & CREAM
¥560

ジェラート あずきストロベリークリーム
GELATO BEAN JAM
STRAWBERRY & CREAM
¥520

ジェラート キャラメルナッツクリーム
GELATO CARAMEL
NUT & CREAM
¥440

ダブルチョコ チーズケーキクリーム
DOUBLE CHOCOLATE
CHEESE CAKE & CREAM
¥560

ジェラート キャラメルチーズケーキクリーム
GELATO CARAMEL
CHEESE CAKE & CREAM
¥530

キウイクリーム
KIWI FRUIT
&CREAM
¥410

ストロベリー チョコクリーム
STRAWBERRY
CHOCOLATE &CREAM
¥410

ベリーベリー
クリーム
BERRY BERRY
& CREAM
¥500

ジェラート ブルーベリークリーム
GELATO BLUEBERRY
& CREAM
¥460

I think desserts are about fun and indulgence. Dessert offers the chance to mess around a bit, to break away from the idea of being sensible and healthy and just go all out. Desserts can have an almost cartoonish element, a sense of playfulness that extends beyond the flavour to colour and texture.

My approach to desserts has been strongly influenced by a trip to Japan where I discovered the things they do with soft serve ice cream. Soft serve is epic there and they come up with some of the kookiest flavour combinations imaginable. It's quite awe inspiring. I first came across it on Shodoshima, an island in Japan's Seto Inland Sea. The main industry there — other than fishing — is the production of soy sauce and there are many brewing facilities on the island. Each of them makes their own distinctive soy sauce and they all have their own shops where they sell bottles of their product. They also sell soy sauce flavoured soft serve. It has a light brown tinge and a really nice savoury element — not salty but savoury and not too sweet. And interestingly, the soft serves in each shop were all slightly different. It was that odd but completely successful hybrid of American and Japanese flavours that has informed the way I have approached desserts ever since.

There are some traditional recipes in this chapter — such as the peanut sesame cookies — but mostly the dishes here are hybrids. The peanut butter parfait that we make at Supernormal is essentially a Western dish, but the nut element means that it sits easily alongside Asian-style desserts.

Some of the desserts here are quite sweet but the sugar levels can be very easily tempered to suit your own taste. You can pull back on the amount of sugar in the recipe because many of them come with sauces and syrups that are quite sweet on their own. Play around a little — it is dessert after all.

JASMINE MARSHMALLOW

Line a 28 x 20 cm (11 x 8 in) plastic tray with baking paper and spray with oil.

Bring 200 ml (7 fl oz) water to the boil and pour it over the tea leaves in a bowl. Leave the tea to infuse for 15 minutes, then strain the tea leaves and discard. Reserve the liquid.

In a small saucepan, heat the caster sugar, honey and tea-infused water and 125 g (4½ oz/1 cup) of the icing sugar to 122°C (252°F).

While the liquid is heating, whisk the egg whites in the bowl of a stand mixer, until they just begin to build in volume.

With the mixer running at high speed, gradually add the sugar syrup, pouring it down the inside of the bowl so that it doesn't splatter off the whisk and stick to the bowl. Add the vanilla bean paste and continue to whisk until combined.

Squeeze the excess water out of the gelatine and put the softened gelatine and 50 ml (1¾ fl oz) of the tea-infused water in a small saucepan over medium heat. Heat gently and stir to dissolve the gelatine.

With the mixer running, pour the liquefied gelatine slowly into the whites as they are whisking. Whisk the mixture until stiff peaks form.

Pour the marshmallow mixture onto the lined tray, using a spatula to spread it into the corners. Wrap the tray entirely in plastic wrap and leave to cool at room temperature.

When cool, cut into squares with a hot knife. Dust the pieces of marshmallow in the remaining icing sugar just before serving.

MAKES ABOUT 60 PIECES

oil for spraying
15 g (½ oz) best-quality jasmine
  tea leaves
250 g (9 oz) caster (superfine) sugar
2 teaspoons honey
2 egg whites
7 gelatine leaves, soaked in
  cold water until soft
½ teaspoon vanilla bean paste
150 g (5½ oz) icing (confectioners') sugar

←
Peanut butter parfait, peanut dacquoise,
chocolate ganache, butterscotch sauce (p.198).

DESSERT

PEANUT BUTTER PARFAIT, PEANUT DACQUOISE, CHOCOLATE GANACHE, BUTTERSCOTCH SAUCE

This is a constant on the menu at Supernormal. It presses all the right buttons, for all the right reasons.

To make the peanut dacquoise, preheat the oven to 170°C (340°F) and line a 30 x 15 cm (12 x 6 in) baking tray with baking paper.

In a bowl, mix together the peanuts, icing sugar and ground almonds.

Whisk the egg whites in an electric mixer until they form soft peaks. While still whisking, gradually sprinkle in the caster sugar and whisk until stiff and glossy. When the whites are ready, transfer them to a large bowl and gently fold the nut mixture through the meringue until combined.

Spread the mixture out on the lined baking tray to a thickness of about 3 mm (⅛ in). Bake for 8 minutes and then turn the tray 180 degrees and return it to the oven for another 8 minutes or until lightly golden. Leave to cool to room temperature.

Line a 30 x 15 x 5 cm (12 x 6 x 2 in) plastic tray with baking paper.

Heat a large saucepan over medium–high heat and scatter 140 g (5 oz) of the sugar over the base. Heat until the sugar melts and starts to colour. Continue to cook, swirling the sugar in the pan occasionally, until you have a light golden caramel, about 2–3 minutes.

Remove the pan from the heat and add 300 ml (10 fl oz) of the cream, half the glucose and the vanilla bean paste. Return to the heat and bring to a simmer, whisking to dissolve any lumps. Add the peanut butter, then the butter and whisk to combine.

Squeeze out any excess water from the softened gelatine leaves, then whisk the gelatine into the hot liquid. Remove the mixture from the heat and strain through a fine sieve into a large bowl.

Put the egg yolks in a stand mixer and whisk until pale and tripled in volume, about 2–3 minutes.

Meanwhile, bring the remaining sugar, glucose and 1½ tablespoons water to the boil in a small saucepan over high heat. Cook until the temperature reaches 117°C (243°F).

With the mixer running on medium speed, pour the hot sugar syrup into the egg yolks in a steady stream. Continue to whisk the eggs for 3 minutes.

Fold the yolk mixture into the peanut butter mixture and cool to room temperature.

SERVES 10
190 g (6½ oz) caster (superfine) sugar
500 ml (17 fl oz/2 cups) pouring (single/light) cream (35% fat), plus 200 ml (7 fl oz) extra pouring cream, whipped to soft peaks
135 g (5 oz) liquid glucose
1 teaspoon vanilla bean paste
75 g (2¾ oz) smooth peanut butter
50 g (1¾ oz) butter, diced
4 gold-strength gelatine leaves, soaked in cold water until soft
9 egg yolks
coarsely crushed roasted peanuts to serve

PEANUT DACQUOISE
70 g (2½ oz) peanuts, roasted then crushed
125 g (4½ oz/1 cup) pure icing (confectioners') sugar, sifted
40 g (1½ oz) ground almonds
80 g (2¾ oz) egg whites (about 2 large egg whites)
50 g (1¾ oz) caster (superfine) sugar

CHOCOLATE GANACHE
2 egg yolks
50 g (1¾ oz) caster (superfine) sugar
50 g (1¾ oz) powdered glucose
100 ml (3½ fl oz) milk
300 ml (10 fl oz) pouring (single/light) cream
250 g (9 oz) dark chocolate (60–70% cocoa solids)

BUTTERSCOTCH SAUCE
115 g (4 oz/½ cup) caster (superfine) sugar
1 teaspoon sea salt
110 g (4 oz) brown sugar
75 ml (2½ fl oz) thickened (whipping) cream
40 g (1½ oz) cold butter, diced

Finally, fold the whipped cream into the peanut mixture and pour it into your prepared tray or individual silicone moulds. Carefully place the dacquoise on top of your parfait (making sure that the smooth bottom of the dacquoise is facing up), cover with plastic wrap and freeze overnight. If using individual moulds, cut rings of the meringue the same size as your silicone moulds.

To make the chocolate ganache, in a bowl, whisk together the egg yolks, sugar and powdered glucose.

In a small saucepan, bring the milk and 100 ml (3½ fl oz) of the cream to the boil. Allow this to cool slightly for 5 minutes then pour it into the egg mixture, whisking as you pour, until thoroughly combined. Return the custard to the saucepan and stir over low heat until it starts to thicken, about 4–6 minutes. Remove from the heat and set aside.

Melt the chocolate in a bowl over a saucepan of simmering water. Do not let the water touch the base of the bowl and do not let the temperature of the chocolate rise above 50°C (122°F). Turn off the heat under the saucepan and mix the custard into the melted chocolate a third at a time.

Whisk the remaining cream to soft peaks and fold it into the chocolate mixture. Transfer to a container with a lid and store in the refrigerator.

To make the butterscotch sauce, heat a saucepan over medium–high heat, scatter the caster sugar over the base and cook until it turns a light golden colour, swirling the pan occasionally to cook evenly. Once the sugar has evenly caramelised to a dark golden colour, reduce the heat and add 50 ml (1¾ fl oz) water to the caramel. Next, whisk in the brown sugar and cream together. Once the brown sugar has dissolved, add the butter and whisk until incorporated. Strain the mixture through a fine sieve and set aside to cool to room temperature. Store in the refrigerator until ready to use.

To serve the peanut butter parfait, remove it from the freezer and turn it out onto a chopping board. Leave it to thaw slightly until it is a workable consistency. When soft enough, cut it into 10 even-sized pieces.

Place a portion of parfait on each serving plate. Spoon a tablespoon of butterscotch sauce over each parfait. Top with some crushed peanuts and 1 tablespoon chocolate ganache.

See photograph (p.196).

TEMPURA-FRIED CUSTARD
WITH GINGER SYRUP

This recipe is a riff on a doughnut concept but the addition of the ginger syrup brings the flavours closer to Asia.

To make the custard, line a 28 x 22 x 3 cm (11 x 8¾ x 1¼ in) plastic tray with baking paper.

Sift the flour and cornflour together into a bowl. Add the sugar and salt.

In a stainless steel saucepan over medium heat, bring the milk, condensed milk, vanilla bean paste and 750 ml (25½ fl oz/3 cups) water to a simmer. Add the dry ingredients to the simmering liquid and whisk continuously. Bring the custard to the boil. Continue to cook until the custard is thick. If you let some custard fall from the whisk back into the pan, you should be able to see the 'ribbons' of custard visible on the surface for a minute or so. When the custard gets to this stage, add the butter and whisk until thoroughly incorporated. Remove from the heat.

Strain the thickened custard into your prepared tray. The custard should be about 2 cm (¾ in) thick. Refrigerate until set, ideally overnight.

To make the ginger syrup, in a stainless steel saucepan over medium heat, bring 250 ml (8½ fl oz/1 cup) water, the sugar and sliced ginger to a simmer and reduce the liquid until you have about 250 ml (8½ fl oz/1 cup) of syrup. Remove from the heat and leave to cool. Once cool, blend the syrup in an upright blender then strain through a fine sieve.

Strain the stem ginger, reserving the syrup for another use. Very finely dice the stem ginger and add it to the cooled syrup. Set aside.

To make the tempura batter, sift the plain flour and cornflour into a bowl.

Whisk the egg yolk into the cold water then whisk this into the flour until quite smooth — a few lumps are okay. Rest the batter in the refrigerator for 30 minutes before using.

Fill a large, heavy-based saucepan one-third full with vegetable oil and heat to 190°C (375°F).

Cut the set custard into 2 cm (¾ in) cubes. Carefully toss the pieces of custard in a little flour until they are lightly coated. Dip them in the tempura batter, one at a time, then drop each piece carefully into the hot oil. Deep-fry the custard (no more than 4 pieces at a time) for 4 minutes or until lightly golden. Drain briefly on paper towel before arranging the fried custard cubes on a serving plate and spooning over a small amount of the ginger syrup.

SERVES 6
vegetable oil for deep-frying
plain (all-purpose) flour for dusting

CUSTARD
2½ tablespoons plain (all-purpose) flour
2 tablespoons cornflour (cornstarch)
230 g (8 oz/1 cup) caster (superfine) sugar
3 teaspoons salt flakes
250 ml (8½ fl oz/1 cup) full-cream (whole) milk
315 ml (10½ fl oz) condensed milk
1 teaspoon vanilla bean paste
60 g (2 oz) butter

GINGER SYRUP
230 g (8 oz/1 cup) caster (superfine) sugar
60 g (2 oz) piece fresh ginger, thinly sliced
1 x 270 g (9½ oz) stem ginger in syrup

TEMPURA BATTER
90 g (3 oz) plain (all-purpose) flour
2 tablespoons cornflour (cornstarch)
1 egg yolk
200 ml (7 fl oz) cold water

↑↑
Team dessert.
↑
Stuff we like: sumo badge.

This tart is best served at room temperature on the day it's made. The recipe makes enough for 2 shells. The remaining pastry can be frozen for later use. Serve with a little bowl of cold whipped cream and a bowl of fresh raspberries.

To make the pastry, put the butter in the bowl of a stand mixer and beat until smooth but not aerated. Add the icing sugar and mix until just combined.

In a separate bowl, combine the egg yolks and cold water. With the mixer running, add this mixture, a little at a time, into the butter mixture. Add the flour and mix on low speed until just combined.

Tip the pastry onto a work surface. Using the heel of your hand, lightly knead the pastry just enough to bring it together in a cohesive mass. Form the pastry into 2 discs. Wrap each disc in plastic wrap and refrigerate until thoroughly chilled, about 1 hour.

Roll one of the pastry discs out to a 5 mm (¼ in) thickness and use it to line a buttered 25 cm (10 in) flan (tart) tin. Place the tart base in the refrigerator for 1 hour to rest.

Preheat the oven to 180°C (350°F).

Carefully line your chilled tart shell with baking paper and fill it with uncooked rice. (The weight of the rice stops the pastry shell from rising as it cooks.) Bake in the oven for about 20 minutes, until golden and cooked through. Remove from the oven and discard the baking paper and rice.

To make the filling, in a bowl, whisk together the eggs, sugar, lime zest and vanilla seeds. Stir in the lime juice, then the cream. Pour the filling into a pitcher.

Reduce the oven temperature to 120°C (250°F).

Pour the filling into the tart, filling it to the brim. Bake for about 20 minutes, checking from time to time, by gently tapping the tin, to see if the filling has set. If the custard does not move or wobble, it is ready. Be vigilant in checking the tart, because once it sets it can very quickly overcook and curdle if not removed from the oven.

SERVES 12

PASTRY
180 g (6½ oz) butter, softened
75 g (2¾ oz) icing
    (confectioners') sugar
2 egg yolks
1 tablespoon cold water
250 g (9 oz/1⅔ cups) plain
    (all-purpose) flour,
    plus extra for dusting

FILLING
6 eggs
200 g (7 oz) sugar
finely grated zest of 2 limes
1 vanilla bean, seeds scraped
200 ml (7 fl oz) lime juice (about 4 limes)
200 ml (7 fl oz) thickened (whipping)
    cream

GINGERBREAD PUDDING,
POACHED PEAR, VANILLA CREAM

This is a dessert that has comfort food as its default position.
It obviously comes from European technique but it also incorporates
flavours you'd find in Asia.

For the poached pears, combine 750 ml (25½ fl oz/3 cups) water, the sugar
and lemon juice in a stainless steel saucepan over low heat. Stir until
the sugar has dissolved. Add the pears and place a round of greaseproof
(waxed) paper on the surface of the poaching liquid to keep the pears
submerged. Simmer very gently for 10–12 minutes or until the pears are
tender. Remove from the heat and leave the pears to cool in the syrup.

To make the vanilla cream, in a medium bowl, whisk together the egg
yolks, sugar, cornflour and vanilla seeds until smooth and well combined.

In a small stainless steel saucepan over medium heat, bring the milk to
a simmer. Whisk one-third of the hot milk into the egg mixture to 'temper'
or stabilise it, then pour the egg mixture back into the pan with the milk,
whisking constantly until the custard has thickened. Pour it into a bowl
and lay a piece of plastic wrap directly on the surface of the custard to
prevent a skin from forming. Refrigerate until cool. When ready to use the
vanilla cream, take 190 ml (6½ fl oz/¾ cup) of the vanilla cream from the
refrigerator and whisk it well to break down any lumps. In another bowl,
whip the cream to soft peaks and fold it into the vanilla cream. Cover and
refrigerate until needed.

Preheat the oven to 170°C (340°F).

In a heavy-based saucepan over medium heat, melt the caster sugar
until it is a golden caramel, then spread 2 tablespoons of this toffee into
each of six 12 cm (4¾ in), lined, heavy-based baking dishes. Alternatively,
use one 28 cm (11 in) ceramic baking dish. Let the caramel set hard.

Slice each poached pear half into 4 wedges. Cut the stem ginger into
thin slices. Distribute the pear and ginger slices evenly on top of the
set caramel.

In a saucepan over medium heat, melt the butter, muscovado sugar,
golden syrup, fresh ginger and cinnamon. Remove from the heat and
leave to cool to room temperature.

In a bowl, whisk together the milk, egg and bicarbonate of soda,
followed by the cooled butter mixture.

Put the flour in a large bowl and whisk in the wet ingredients until well
combined. Pour 80 ml (2½ fl oz/⅓ cup) of this gingerbread mixture evenly
over the ginger and pear in the lined pans. Bake for 20–22 minutes until
just cooked. Serve with the vanilla cream.

SERVES 6
250 g (9 oz) caster (superfine) sugar
8 pieces stem ginger in syrup, drained
75 g (2¾ oz) butter
60 g (2 oz) dark muscovado sugar
200 g (7 oz) golden syrup
   (light corn syrup)
1 teaspoon finely grated fresh ginger
1 teaspoon ground cinnamon
125 ml (4 fl oz/½ cup) milk
1 egg
½ teaspoon bicarbonate of soda
   (baking soda), dissolved in 80 ml
   (2½ fl oz/⅓ cup) warm water
150 g (5½ oz/1 cup) plain
   (all-purpose) flour

POACHED PEARS
230 g (8 oz/1 cup firmly packed)
   brown sugar
60 ml (2 fl oz/¼ cup) lemon juice
3 beurre bosc pears, peeled,
   halved and cored

VANILLA CREAM
2 egg yolks
3 tablespoons caster (superfine) sugar
2 teaspoons cornflour (cornstarch)
2 vanilla beans, seeds scraped
250 ml (8½ fl oz/1 cup) milk
250 ml (8½ fl oz/1 cup) pouring
   (single/light) cream

↑
Pastry section.
→
Gingerbread pudding, poached pear,
vanilla cream (p.205).

BAKED MERINGUE, ROSE WATER CREAM, LYCHEE SORBET

To make the lychee sorbet, put the lime juice, sugar and inverted sugar syrup in a small stainless steel saucepan over medium heat and bring to a simmer. Remove the pan from the heat and leave to cool.

In an upright blender, purée the lychees with the cooled syrup until smooth. Strain the mixture through a fine sieve then churn in an ice cream maker according to the manufacturer's instructions.

To make the rose water cream, in a small stainless steel saucepan over medium heat, bring the milk to a simmer. Add the jasmine tea, remove the pan from the heat, cover with a lid and leave to infuse for 30 minutes.

In a medium bowl, whisk the egg yolk and sugar until thick and pale. Whisk in the cornflour and vanilla.

Strain the milk and pour it into a clean saucepan over medium heat then bring it back to a simmer.

Whisk a little of the hot milk into the egg mixture to 'temper' them before adding the rest of the milk, whisking well. Return the mixture to the pan over medium heat, stirring constantly until the custard has thickened.

Remove from the heat and place in the refrigerator to cool, covering the surface of the custard with plastic wrap to prevent a skin forming.

Using an electric mixer, whisk the cream to soft peaks and fold in 125 ml (4 fl oz/½ cup) of the custard along with the rose water. Cover and refrigerate until needed.

To make the raspberry gel, in a small stainless steel saucepan over medium heat, bring the raspberries, sugar and lemon juice to a simmer. When the raspberries have softened and collapsed, remove the pan from the heat and strain the mixture through a fine sieve.

Put the liquid in a clean saucepan along with 2 teaspoons water and bring to the boil. Once boiling, add the agar agar and whisk continuously for 1 minute. Remove from the heat and cool in the refrigerator. Once cool, add the rose water and mix thoroughly with a wooden spoon until smooth. If lumps have developed, strain the sauce through a fine sieve.

SERVES 6
3 egg whites
pinch of salt
170 g (6 oz/¾ cup) caster (superfine) sugar
40 g (1½ oz/¼ cup) freeze-dried raspberries to serve

LYCHEE SORBET
2½ tablespoons lime juice
75 g (2¾ oz) caster (superfine) sugar
1 tablespoon inverted sugar syrup (available from specialty baking shops or online)
1 x 400 g (14 oz) tin lychees

ROSE WATER CREAM
250 ml (8½ fl oz/1 cup) milk
½ teaspoon jasmine tea leaves
1 egg yolk
3 tablespoons caster (superfine) sugar
3 teaspoons cornflour (cornstarch)
½ teaspoon vanilla bean paste
250 ml (8½ fl oz/1 cup) pouring (single/light) cream
¼ teaspoon rose water

RASPBERRY GEL
100 g (3½ oz/⅔ cup) frozen raspberries
2½ tablespoons caster (superfine) sugar
1½ tablespoons lemon juice
½ teaspoon agar agar
½ teaspoon rose water

Preheat the oven to 140°C (275°F) and line a baking tray with baking paper.

In the bowl of a stand mixer, whisk the egg whites with the salt. As the whites begin to build in volume, gradually add half the sugar. Whisk for another minute or until the whites are glossy and stiff. Using a spatula, fold the remaining half of the sugar through the egg whites.

With a large kitchen spoon, scoop equal-sized (about ¼ cup) meringues onto the lined baking tray. Bake for 1 hour, checking the meringues from time to time. If the meringues start to colour before they are cooked, reduce the temperature a little. When cooked, remove the meringues from the oven and leave to cool.

To serve, dollop a spoonful of raspberry gel onto each serving plate and top with a meringue. Place 2 spoonfuls of rose water cream on top of each meringue, followed by a scoop of lychee sorbet. Finish by crushing the freeze-dried raspberries over the whole dessert.

See photograph (p.210).

↑
The 25-metre bar.
←
Baked meringue, rose water cream, lychee sorbet (p.208).

POACHED MERINGUE, PINK PEPPERCORN MERINGUE, SHEEP'S MILK YOGHURT CREAM, SHISO GRANITA

The shiso granita brings an unexpected, refreshing, aromatic element to this dessert.

To make the shiso granita, heat 190 ml (6½ fl oz/¾ cup) water and the sugar in a small saucepan over medium heat, stirring, until the sugar has dissolved. Set aside to cool.

Bring a saucepan of water to the boil. Blanch the shiso leaves for 30 seconds then cool them in iced water. Strain them, squeeze out any excess water and place the leaves in an upright blender. Add the cooled sugar syrup and blend on high speed until the syrup is dark green.

Pass the syrup through a fine sieve, then pour it into a shallow plastic tray. Place in the freezer, stirring with a fork every 10 minutes, breaking up any ice crystals as they develop. Continue until your granita is frozen and has a light, flaky texture.

To make the pink peppercorn meringue, preheat the oven to 100°C (210°F). Line a baking tray with baking paper.

In the bowl of a stand mixer, whisk the egg white until foamy. While still whisking, sprinkle in the sugars, salt and white pepper. Whisk until the meringue is thick and glossy, then spread it out on the lined baking tray to a thickness of about 3 mm (¼ in). Sprinkle the crushed pink peppercorns evenly over the top. Bake in the oven for 3 hours. Turn off the oven and leave to cool for another 2 hours. Alternatively you can use a dehydrator.

To make the sheep's milk yoghurt cream, put the yoghurt in a colander lined with muslin (cheesecloth) set over another bowl. Transfer to the refrigerator and leave for 2 hours or until the yoghurt has thickened. Discard the liquid.

In a medium bowl, whip the cream with the sugar and vanilla. Fold the yoghurt into the cream and leave in the refrigerator until needed.

In the bowl of a stand mixer, whisk the egg whites with the egg white powder until soft peaks form. With the mixer running, gradually sprinkle in the caster sugar and whisk until the mixture forms stiff peaks. Turn the mixer down to a low speed and mix in the vanilla and lemon zest until well combined.

Use two spoons to make 6–8 cm (2½–3¾ in) egg shapes, or quenelles, out of the meringue.

MAKES ABOUT 12 MERINGUES
(6–8 CM/2½–3¼ IN LONG)

75 g (2¾ oz) egg whites
  (about 2½ egg whites)
5 g (¼ oz) (about 1 teaspoon)
  egg white powder
75 g (2¾ oz) caster (superfine) sugar,
  plus 1 extra tablespoon
¼ teaspoon vanilla bean paste
¼ teaspoon lemon zest
½ teaspoon lemon juice
1 fuji apple

SHISO GRANITA
55 g (2 oz/¼ cup) sugar
20g (¾ oz/1 cup firmly packed)
  shiso leaves

PINK PEPPERCORN MERINGUE
1 egg white
2 tablespoons icing
  (confectioners') sugar
2 tablespoons caster (superfine) sugar
pinch of salt
pinch of ground white pepper
1 tablespoon finely crushed pink
peppercorns, sifted

SHEEP'S MILK YOGHURT CREAM
150 g (5½ oz) sheep's milk yoghurt
2 tablespoons pouring
  (single/light) cream
1 tablespoon caster (superfine) sugar
¼ teaspoon vanilla bean paste

POACHED MERINGUE, PINK PEPPERCORN MERINGUE,
SHEEP'S MILK YOGHURT CREAM, SHISO GRANITA (CONTINUED)

Place the meringues onto small rounds of baking paper that fit
comfortably into your steamer (approximately 4 meringues per
steamer basket).

Steam the meringues over boiling water for about 5 minutes with the
lid on. Break one open to see if it is cooked all the way through. It should
not be runny and should look firm. (If the meringues puff up, this means
your steamer is too hot and the meringue has overcooked.) Once the
meringues are cooked, transfer them to a tray lined with baking paper
and leave to cool at room temperature before refrigerating.

In a small saucepan over medium heat, combine 60 ml (2 fl oz/¼ cup)
water with the extra tablespoon caster sugar and heat until the sugar
has dissolved. Remove from the heat and allow to cool, then add the
lemon juice.

Peel the apple and dice it into 5 mm (¼ in) cubes. Put the cubes in
the sugar syrup immediately so they don't discolour.

To serve, place a large spoonful of yoghurt cream on a serving plate,
followed by a poached meringue and 1 tablespoon of apple pieces.
Scatter over 2 tablespoons of shiso granita and finish by crushing
the pink peppercorn meringue over the entire dish.

See photograph (p.214).

↑
Poached meringue, pink peppercorn meringue,
sheep's milk yoghurt cream, shiso granita (p.212).
→
Pastry chef Amy and meringues.

PEANUT AND SESAME COOKIES

Preheat the oven to 180°C (350°F) and line a baking tray with baking paper.

In the bowl of a stand mixer, cream the butter and sugars together. Add the peanut butter and mix well. Finally, add the flour and baking powder, stirring until just combined.

Put the sesame seeds on a plate or a sheet of baking paper.

Turn the cookie mixture out onto a work surface, roll it into a 4 cm (1½ in) diameter log and then roll it in the sesame seeds. Wrap the dough in plastic wrap and place it in the refrigerator to firm up.

Once firm, slice the dough into 5 mm (¼ in) discs. Place the cookies on the lined baking tray and bake for 12–14 minutes or until golden.

MAKES 20 COOKIES

200 g (7 oz) butter,
   at room temperature
120 g (4½ oz) caster (superfine) sugar
120 g (4½ oz) brown sugar
200 g (7 oz) smooth peanut butter
320 g (11½ oz) plain (all-purpose) flour,
   sifted, plus extra for dusting
8 g (¼ oz) baking powder
40 g (1½ oz/¼ cup) sesame seeds

BLACK PEPPER SAUCE

MAKES ABOUT 1 CUP

3 red Asian shallots, finely chopped
2.5 cm (1 in) piece fresh ginger, finely chopped
4 garlic cloves, finely chopped
60 ml (2 fl oz/¼ cup) grapeseed oil
2 long red chillies, seeded and finely chopped
2 teaspoons black peppercorns, roughly ground
2 teaspoons sugar
1 tablespoon sweet soy sauce
1 tablespoon dark soy sauce
1 tablespoon light soy sauce
2 teaspoons rice wine vinegar

In a stainless steel saucepan over medium heat, gently fry the shallots, ginger and garlic in the grapeseed oil for 3–4 minutes until aromatic and wilted. Add the chilli and black pepper and continue to cook for a further 2 minutes. Add the sugar and the sweet, dark and light soy sauces and bring to the boil.

Remove the pan from the heat and set aside to cool. Once cool stir in the rice wine vinegar. Store in an airtight container in the refrigerator for up to 3 days.

↑
Black pepper sauce.

PLUM SAUCE

MAKES 1 LITRE (34 FL OZ/4 CUPS)

500 g (1 lb 2 oz) tinned blood plums, pips removed and liquid reserved
435 ml (15 fl oz/1¾ cups) cider vinegar
½ teaspoon black pepper
2 teaspoons ground cloves
1 tablespoon sea salt flakes
½ teaspoon cayenne pepper
5 cm (2 in) piece fresh ginger, grated
220 g (8 oz/1 cup) sugar

In a large stainless steel saucepan over medium–high heat, combine all the ingredients, including the reserved blood plum liquid, but omitting the sugar. Bring the mixture to the boil then reduce the heat to low and simmer gently for 1½ hours or until thickened.

Add the sugar and cook for a further 20 minutes over low heat. Remove from the heat and leave to cool. Once cool, blend the sauce in an upright blender then pass it through a fine sieve. Store in an airtight container for up to 1 week.

YUXIANG SAUCE

This is a very versatile sauce. It's delicious spooned over cold roast pork as a cold cut to start a meal or tossed with cold cooked chicken and cucumber to make a striking salad.

MAKES 1 CUP

2 tablespoons vegetable oil
6 spring onions (scallions), white part only, thinly sliced
6 garlic cloves, finely chopped
2 tablespoons finely chopped fresh ginger
30 g (1 oz) sugar
1 heaped teaspoon ground Sichuan peppercorns
1 teaspoon ground black peppercorns
80 ml (2½ fl oz/⅓ cup) light soy sauce
80 ml (2½ fl oz/⅓ cup) Chinese black vinegar (Chinkiang vinegar)
1 tablespoon black bean chilli paste

Heat the oil in a saucepan over medium heat and sauté the spring onion, garlic and ginger until soft and aromatic, stirring constantly. Add the sugar and both peppers and cook for a further 2 minutes. Reduce the heat to low and add the soy sauce, vinegar and chilli paste. Bring to a simmer and immediately remove the pan from the heat and allow to cool. Store in the refrigerator until ready to use. It will keep for up to a week.

BLACK BEAN SAUCE

This is a great version of the classic Cantonese sauce. It's versatile, great with vegetables and seafood, and will keep well in the refrigerator for up to a week.

MAKES 625 ML (21 FL OZ/2½ CUPS)

60 ml (2 fl oz/¼ cup) grapeseed oil
7.5 cm (3 in) piece fresh ginger, finely shredded
12 garlic cloves, finely diced
⅓ cup salted black beans, soaked in water for 10 minutes
80 ml (2½ fl oz/⅓ cup) Shaoxing rice wine
250 ml (8½ fl oz/1 cup) best-quality oyster sauce
1 tablespoon sweet soy sauce
1 tablespoon sesame oil

In a stainless steel saucepan over medium heat, gently warm the grapeseed oil. Add the ginger and cook for 3–4 minutes until aromatic and wilted. Add the garlic and continue to cook until the garlic is soft.

Meanwhile, strain and finely chop the black beans.

Add the Shaoxing rice wine to the ginger and garlic and simmer until reduced by half.

Add the oyster sauce, 190 ml (6½ fl oz/¾ cup) water, the black beans and sweet soy sauce and bring to a simmer. Continue to cook, stirring occasionally, for 10 minutes. If the sauce seems a little thick, thin it with a few tablespoons of water.

Remove from the heat and stir in the sesame oil once the sauce has cooled.

XO SAUCE

XO sauce was created in Hong Kong. It's made from premium ingredients and was named after XO Cognac, which is much loved and revered in Hong Kong. It's available ready made but the freshly made stuff will beat the stuff in a jar every time.

MAKES ABOUT 1½ CUPS

25 g (1 oz) dried scallops
75 g (2¾ oz) dried shrimp
125 ml (4 fl oz/½ cup) vegetable oil
5 red Asian shallots, thinly sliced
15 garlic cloves, sliced
50 g (1¾ oz) jamón or prosciutto, finely chopped
6 fresh long red chillies, seeded and finely chopped
6 dried long red chillies, seeded, soaked in water for 30 minutes, and finely chopped
10 dried bird's eye chillies, finely chopped
1 teaspoon roasted shrimp paste
3 teaspoons sugar, or to taste

Soak the dried scallops and dried shrimp separately, each in 125 ml (4 fl oz/½ cup) hot water, until they are plump (about 1 hour).

Drain the scallops and reserve the soaking water. Tear the drained scallops into fine shreds, pat dry on paper towel and set aside.

Drain the prawns and reserve the soaking water. Finely chop the prawns and set aside.

Heat the oil in a wok or large saucepan over medium–high heat. Add the shallots and garlic, cooking until pale golden in colour.

Add the scallops and dried shrimp and stir continuously until golden brown, about 4–5 minutes.

Stir through the jamón and fresh and dried chillies, frying for 1 minute before adding the shrimp paste, sugar and reserved scallop and shrimp water.

Reduce the heat to medium and cook, stirring occasionally, until the sauce is fragrant and the water has completely evaporated, about 10–20 minutes.

Remove from the heat and strain, reserving the oil. Transfer the solids to a sterilised jar, then pour in enough of the reserved oil to cover. XO sauce will keep refrigerated in a sealed container for 1 month.

SPRING ONION OIL

MAKES 125 ML (4 FL OZ/½ CUP)
125 ml (4 fl oz/½ cup) grapeseed oil
100 g (3½ oz) green spring onion
   (scallion) tops, roughly chopped

Heat the oil in a saucepan to 70°C (160°F). Add the spring onion and remove the pan from the heat. Leave to cool for 3 minutes.

Transfer to an upright blender and purée for 2 minutes at high speed. Set aside in the refrigerator to cool. Leave for 1 hour before straining through a fine sieve. Store in an airtight container in the refrigerator for up to 2 days.

GARLIC OIL

MAKES 60 ML (2 FL OZ/¼ CUP)
1 garlic clove, thinly sliced
60 ml (2 fl oz/¼ cup) grapeseed oil

Fry the garlic in the oil in a small saucepan until the garlic is deep golden in colour. Strain, discard the garlic and cool the oil. This is best used fresh but will keep in an airtight container for 2 days.

MISO DRESSING

MAKES 125 ML (4 FL OZ/½ CUP)
2 cm (¾ in) piece fresh ginger, thinly sliced
60 ml (2 fl oz/¼ cup) grapeseed oil
1 tablespoon rice wine vinegar
3 teaspoons white miso paste
½ ripe nashi, peeled, cored and chopped
¼ teaspoon salt
pinch of ground white pepper

In a small saucepan over medium–low heat, fry the ginger in the grapeseed oil until the ginger is golden. Strain the oil and set aside to cool. Discard the ginger.

Put the vinegar, miso, nashi, salt and pepper in an upright blender and process until smooth. With the blender running, slowly pour in the cooled ginger oil to emulsify the dressing. Check the seasoning and correct if needed. Store in an airtight container for up to 3 days.

PONZU BASE

A great base recipe that's indispensable in a lot of our recipes. Bottled ponzu is available in stores, but it lacks the vibrancy the fresh fruit brings.

MAKES 1 CUP
½ lemon
½ lime
¼ grapefruit
1 orange
125 ml (4 fl oz/½ cup) light soy sauce
2 tablespoons yuzu juice
5 x 5 cm (2 x 2 in) piece kombu

Wash all of the citrus fruit and dry well. Slice the fruit thinly and place it in a container. Add the soy sauce, yuzu juice and kombu. Leave for at least 3 hours or overnight.

Remove the citrus from the container with a slotted spoon and squeeze as much of the liquid from the fruit back into the container as you can. Discard the fruit. Taste and adjust with a little more soy sauce if it's too sour.

Pass the ponzu through a fine strainer and store in the refrigerator.

PICKLED GINGER

MAKES ABOUT 2 CUPS
175 g (6 oz) young fresh ginger
3 teaspoons salt
125 ml (4 fl oz/½ cup) rice vinegar
110 g (4 oz/½ cup) sugar

Peel the ginger then slice it thinly using a mandoline.

In a medium bowl, mix 1 teaspoon of the salt with 500 ml (17 fl oz/2 cups) water. Add the ginger and steep for 1 hour, stirring from time to time.

Strain the ginger and rinse it under running water. Press any excess water out of the ginger, pat it dry and set it aside it in a heatproof container.

In a small saucepan over medium heat, put the vinegar, sugar, remaining salt and 125 ml (4 fl oz/½ cup) water. Cook until the sugar has dissolved, taking care not to let it boil.

Once the sugar has dissolved, pour the liquid over the ginger. Leave to pickle for at least 1 week before use. Store in the refrigerator for 3 months.

↑
Pickled ginger.

SWEET GINGER DRESSING

MAKES 100 ML (3½ FL OZ)
2 teaspoons sweet ginger vinegar
2 teaspoons pickled ginger liquid
   (see recipe this page)
1 tablespoon white soy sauce
¾ teaspoon rice vinegar
60 ml (2 fl oz/¼ cup) grapeseed oil

Whisk all the ingredients together in a small bowl. Store in an airtight container for up to 2 days.

KIMCHI

This recipe was given to us by my good friend Paul Lee. Paul imports traditional and artisanal products from Korea and is one of our favourite suppliers.

MAKES ABOUT 2 KG (4 LB 6 OZ)
1 Chinese cabbage (wombok)
2 tablespoons salt

KIMCHI BASE
5 cm (2 in) piece kombu
2 tablespoons glutinous (sticky) rice,
   soaked in water overnight
1 tablespoon glutinous (sticky) rice flour
5 spring onions (scallions),
   white part only, halved lengthways
   then cut into 4 cm (1½ in) lengths
60 g (2 oz/¾ cup) Korean chilli flakes
7 dried bird's eye chillies, soaked in water
   for 30 minutes, finely chopped
1 thumb-sized piece fresh ginger,
   finely chopped
10 garlic cloves, finely chopped

1 nashi, peeled and cut into 1.5 mm (⅛ in) batons
80 ml (2½ fl oz/⅓ cup) good-quality fish sauce
1 tablespoon anchovy sauce
2 tablespoons dried fish
2 tablespoons fermented shrimp, finely chopped
60 ml (2 fl oz/¼ cup) fermented plum extract
2 teaspoons caster (superfine) sugar

To make the kimchi base, put 125 ml (4 fl oz/ ½cup) water and the kombu in a saucepan over medium heat. Cook until just under boiling point, then remove the pan from the heat and set aside to cool.

Strain the soaked rice. Put the rice and rice flour in an upright blender with 60 ml (2 fl oz/¼ cup) of the kombu water and blend until smooth.

Transfer to a small saucepan over low heat and cook until thick and gluey, about 5 minutes. Remove from the heat and set aside to cool.

Put all the kimchi base ingredients in a large bowl and, wearing latex gloves, mix until well combined. Set aside.

Make a 5 cm (2 in) cut from the base of the cabbage up into the stem, but not all the way through. Possibly using a knife for initial leverage, work your fingers into the cut and gently pull the cabbage into 2 halves. This prevents shredding the delicate inner leaves.

Mix together the salt and 80 ml (2½ fl oz/ ⅓ cup) water.

Working over a large bowl, brush the salt water over the cabbage, leaf by leaf, taking care not to damage the cabbage. Place the cabbage, face up, in a plastic container and pour over any remaining salt water. Leave to soak for 3 hours.

Turn the cabbage over and leave for another 3 hours.

Remove and rinse under water 3 times. Lightly squeeze out the cabbage and leave to drain in a colander.

In a large bowl take one half of cabbage and, wearing gloves, start at the outer leaves and coat each leaf in the kimchi base, making sure each leaf is well covered and the cabbage remains intact. Continue with the rest of the cabbage and repeat with the other half.

Pick up and hold a cabbage half in one hand, fold the outer leaves over and into the inner leaves, as if you're wrapping a baby up in a blanket.

Place carefully into a plastic container. Top the cabbage with any remaining kimchi base and press down lightly. Cover with a lid and leave at room temperature for 24 hours. Place in the refrigerator for 3 weeks, tasting after 2 weeks. This will keep for 2 months in the refrigerator.

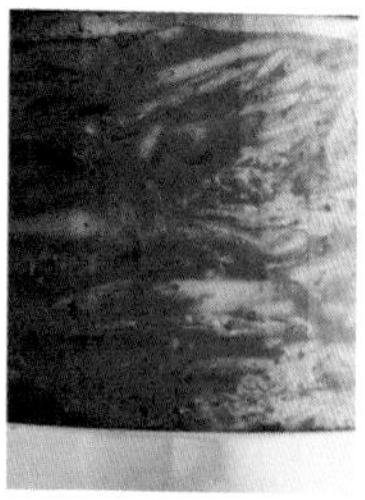

↑
Kimchi.

PICKLED CABBAGE

This is a great pickle recipe, which I like to eat and serve with roast meat or at the start of a meal.

MAKES 1 LITRE

½ savoy cabbage
2 tablespoons sea salt
½ dried long red chilli, seeded
½ teaspoon white peppercorns, crushed
½ fresh long red chilli, seeded and thinly sliced
500 ml (17 fl oz/2 cups) rice wine vinegar
230 g (8 oz/1 cup) caster (superfine) sugar

Cut the cabbage into large chunks and place it in a colander. Rinse under cold running water, then drain well.

In a large bowl, mix the sea salt through the cabbage, then leave it to cure for 3 hours in a colander set over a large bowl.

Preheat the oven to 180°C (350°F).

Put the dried chillies and peppercorns in a small ovenproof dish and roast them for 2 minutes, or until the dried chilli has blackened slightly and the peppercorns are fragrant.

Transfer the spices to a mortar and pestle and pound until coarsely ground.

Squeeze the cabbage in your hands to extract all the liquid you can. Discard the liquid and transfer the cabbage to a large bowl. Sprinkle over the spice mixture with the fresh chilli.

Heat the vinegar and sugar in a stainless steel saucepan over medium heat, and stir until the sugar has dissolved. Bring to the boil and then pour the hot pickling liquid over the cabbage. Mix well so that the spices are evenly distributed. Cool to room temperature, then refrigerate. Leave for at least 1 week to pickle. Store for 4 weeks in the refrigerator.

PICKLED FENNEL

A great snack to start a meal or a wonderful accompaniment to raw fish.

MAKES ABOUT 2 CUPS

125 ml (4 fl oz/½ cup) rice wine vinegar
75 g (2¾ oz/⅓ cup) sugar
1 tablespoon salt
2 tablespoons yuzu juice
1 large fennel bulb

In a small saucepan over medium heat, put the vinegar, 250 ml (8½ fl oz/1 cup) water, the sugar and salt and cook until the sugar has dissolved, taking care not to let it boil. Remove the pan from the heat and set aside to cool to room temperature.

When the mixture is cool add the yuzu juice. Set this pickling liquid aside.

Trim the stalks from the top of the fennel and cut the bulb in half. Using a mandoline, shave the fennel lengthways as thinly as possible then transfer it to a bowl. Pour the cold pickling liquid over the fennel, cover and refrigerate for at least 2 hours, or overnight, before using. Store in the refrigerator for up to 2 weeks.

PICKLED CHILLI

MAKES 1 CUP

6 long red chillies, halved lengthways and seeded
60 ml (2 fl oz/¼ cup) rice wine vinegar
2 tablespoons sugar
2 teaspoons salt

Put the chillies in a bowl.

In a small saucepan over medium heat, put the vinegar, 125 ml (4 fl oz/½ cup) water, the sugar and salt and cook until the sugar has dissolved, taking care not to let it boil.

Remove the pan from the heat and pour the pickling liquid over the chillies. Leave overnight to marinate. Drain.

In an upright blender, purée the chillies with a little of the pickling liquid until smooth. Store in the refrigerator.

FERMENTED CHILLI

This recipe makes a sauce similar to sriracha sauce found in most Asian grocery stores. We go to the trouble of making it ourselves because the fresh fermented sauce has a more vibrant, pungent flavour than the store-bought product. It works particularly well spooned onto freshly shucked oysters.

MAKES ABOUT 1 LITRE (34 FL OZ/4 CUPS)
1 kg (2 lb 3 oz) red jalapeños
5 garlic cloves
250 ml (8½ fl oz/1 cup) white vinegar

In a food processor, process the jalapeños and garlic to a rough pulp. Weigh the pulp and add 3% of its weight in salt to the mixture, stirring to combine thoroughly.

Transfer the mixture to an airtight plastic container and leave to ferment at room temperature for at least 4 days.

On the fifth day, place the mixture in the refrigerator for 24 hours.

The following day, purée the chilli mixture and vinegar in a blender until smooth and then strain into a saucepan. Bring to a simmer over medium heat. Reduce the heat to low and cook until it thickens, stirring regularly as it easily catches on the bottom of the pan. When thickened, remove the pan from the heat and set aside to cool. Transfer to a sterilised jar and store in the refrigerator.

↑
Fermented chilli.

PICKLED SHALLOTS

MAKES ABOUT ⅓ CUP
6 red Asian shallots, thinly sliced
60 ml (2 fl oz/¼ cup) rice wine vinegar
2 tablespoons sugar
2 teaspoons salt

Put the shallots in a bowl.

In a small saucepan over medium heat, warm the remaining ingredients with 125 ml (4 fl oz/ ½ cup) water until the sugar has dissolved, taking care not to let it boil. Remove the pan from the heat and let it cool for 10 minutes.

Pour the pickling liquid over the shallots and leave them to pickle for at least 2 hours before serving. Use immediately.

FRIED SHALLOTS

MAKES ABOUT ½ CUP
500 ml (17 fl oz/2 cups) grapeseed oil
6 red Asian shallots, thinly sliced

In a large, heavy-based saucepan, heat the oil to 160°C (320°F).

Meanwhile, set a sieve over a similar-sized pan and line a tray with paper towel.

Add the sliced shallots to the oil, stirring continuously. When the shallots are lightly golden in colour, pour the shallots into the sieve and drain well. Tip the shallots out onto the tray and use a fork to separate them, which also helps to cool them down. Store in an airtight container for 1–2 days.

FURIKAKE

Furikake is an umami packed seasoning that's usually sprinkled over rice. It's available in most Asian grocery stores. We like to make our own for its freshness. This recipe is our own unique Supernormal blend.

MAKES ¼ CUP
1 orange
1 tablespoon sesame seeds
1 teaspoon black sesame seeds
1 sheet nori
5 g (¼ oz) shaved kombu
5 g (¼ oz) (about 4 tablespoons) shaved bonito
1½ teaspoons puffed wild rice

Preheat the oven to 100°C (210°F).

Zest the orange directly onto a tray lined with baking paper. Put the tray in the oven and dehydrate the orange zest for about 1 hour.

When the orange zest is dry, take it out of the oven and set aside.

Increase the oven temperature to 160°C (320°F). Toast both kinds of sesame seeds in the oven for 5 minutes or until the white sesame seeds are golden. Remove from the oven and set aside.

Meanwhile spread the nori, kombu and bonito out on another baking tray lined with baking paper. Turn the oven off and place the tray in the oven. Leave for 2–3 minutes to gently toast the nori, kombu and bonito.

Using a mortar and pestle or an electric spice grinder, grind the dried orange zest and puffed wild rice to a coarse powder. Crush the nori into small pieces. Mix all the ingredients together in a bowl and gently crush them with your hand.

↑
Furikake.

A SIMPLE MENU

Soy-roasted pumpkin seeds (p.41)

↑

Tomato salad, tofu, yuzu kosho (p.157)

Rib eye with black pepper sauce (p.185)

Chrysanthemum leaf salad with ginger and sesame dressing (p.143)

Peanut and sesame cookies (p.217)

COCKTAIL PARTY

Sesame cucumbers (p.44)

Devilled crab (p.60)

Tuna, avocado, wakame, pickled cucumber (p.73)

Chicken heart and thigh with yakitori sauce (p.87)

Lobster roll (p.159)

Grilled lamb ribs (p.55)

Potsticker dumplings (p.121)

Twice cooked duck legs, plum sauce, steamed bread (p.177)

↑

Beef intercostals with Korean chilli dressing (p.85)

Tempura-fried custard with ginger syrup (p.201)

PICNIC

Kohlrabi kimchi (p.49)

Pickled fennel (p.220)

Silken tofu, marinated eggplant, Yuxiang sauce (p.147)

Homemade mung bean noodles, white cut chicken, roasted sesame dressing (p.83)

↑

Pork tonkatsu sandwiches (p.97)

Jasmine marshmallow (p.195)

DINNER WITH THE KIDS

Candied walnuts with toasted nori (p.39)

Fried rice with crab (p.103)

↑

Prawn and chicken dumplings with spiced vinegar (on the side!) (p.125)

Baby corn with miso butter (p.151)

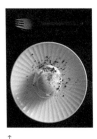
↑

Baked meringue, rose water cream, lychee sorbet (p.208)

WEEKNIGHT DINNER

Marinated cucumber and radish (p.45)

↑

Sea bream, daikon, sweet ginger dressing (p.75)

Spicy minced pork, eggplant, rice noodles, Sichuan sauce (p.183)

Chrysanthemum leaf salad with ginger and sesame dressing (p.143)

Lime and vanilla bean tart (p.203)

FORMAL DINNER PARTY

Sesame cucumbers (p.44)

Pickled shiitake mushrooms (p.59)

Seaweed crackers, uni, pickled shallots (p.65)

↑

Rolled pork, white kimchi, Yuxiang sauce (p.93)

Lobster roll (p.159)

Spinach and tofu dumplings (p.119)

Whole roast lamb shoulder, coriander and mint paste, Sichuan sauce (p.191)

Peas, mustard leaf, XO sauce (p.139)

Peanut butter parfait, peanut dacquoise, chocolate ganache, butterscotch sauce (p.198)

p.24
One of the first objects Andrew
bought while in Japan, Nobuyoshi
Araki's **The Banquet (Shokuji)**, 1993.

p.27
Set custard, prior to being fried.

p.31
Pressed pig's head.

p.88

p.90

p.91

p.92

p.94

p.95

p.96

p.98

p.100

p.101

p.102

p.106

p.108

p.110

p.114

p.115

p.116

p.118

p.120

p.123

p.124

p.126

p.127

p.128

p.130

p.131

p.134

p.135

p.136

p.140

p.144

p.145

p.148

p.152

p.154

p.156

p.158

p.160

p.160

p.162

p.164

p.165

p.166

p.168

p.170

p.172

p.174

p.176

p.178

p.179

p.180

p.182

p.184

p.185

p.188

p.189

p.190

p.192

p.194

p.196

p.197   p.200   p.202   p.202   p.204   p.206

p.207   p.210   p.211   p.214   p.215   p.216

p.218   p.219   p.220   p.221   p.221   p.235

Endpaper (back)

01
CIBI
CIBI is the love and life's work of Meg and Zenta Tanaka, who blend their training and experience in food and wine, design and architecture with a Japanese sensibility. From their upbringing and their evolving life in Australia, they have created a unique lifestyle experience, summed up by their philosophy: head, hands, heart. CIBI operates as a café, gallery and store, stocking unique Japanese design objects, textiles and everyday wares.

02
CLAMMS SEAFOOD
Clamms Seafood is one of the best and longest established wholesale seafood suppliers in Melbourne. Owners Con and James Andronis and George Kaparos source produce from wholesale markets and directly through ports and fishermen, aquaculture farms and credible suppliers across Australia.

03
MOONLIGHT FLAT OYSTERS
Steve and Reni Feletti own and operate Moonlight Flat Oysters on the Clyde River, near Batemans Bay on the south coast of New South Wales. They offer a range of trademarked brands driven by the philosophy of well-raised oysters that are hand chosen and delivered by the fastest farm-direct logistics. Their oyster farms are chemical-free at every stage of growing, harvesting and packing. Steve has pioneered a method of oyster affinage or 'finishing' in Australia, which gives Moonlight Flat oysters their unique texture and flavour profile.

04
MEATSMITH
Offering both wholesale and retail heritage meats, Meatsmith is co-owned by Andrew McConnell and Troy Wheeler. Both are passionate about best-quality heritage meats and skilled butchery. The business focuses on partnering with dedicated producers who raise ethically reared breeds and produce meat that deserves to be celebrated. Meatsmith specialises in onsite butchery, drawing on Troy's 20+ years' experience.

05
THE MELBOURNE PANTRY
Father and son team David (senior) and David (junior) Freeman bring their best British techniques to the finest Australian produce. They combine traditional training with unique cold-smoking methods to craft British-style cold-smoked meats.

06
TABLE 181
Idylle Lee owns and operates Table 181, offering imported specialty Korean and Japanese ingredients for the Australian wholesale market.

07
JONELLA FARM
Based in West Gippsland, Jonella Farm has been growing vegetables for nearly 40 years. Their soil is rich and heavy, ideal for growing high-quality, delicious vegetables. They use crop rotation methods to grow sweet corn, baby corn, pumpkin (squash), asparagus, snow peas (mangetout), broad (fava) beans and green beans.

08
SARA SCHREURS
Established in 1964, the Schreurs family farm has over 40 years' experience in growing vegetables, specialising in leeks, parsnip, baby cos (romaine), endive (chicory), Chinese cabbage (wombok), kohlrabi and radicchio. They utilise sustainable practices and harness the best methods from conventional farming, organics and biodynamics.

09
SHIMA WASABI
Shima Wasabi have been researching and perfecting the art of growing authentic Japanese wasabi (Wasabia japonica) in Australia for over 12 years and are now the largest producer of fresh wasabi in the southern hemisphere. They use climate-controlled greenhouses and a unique hydroponic production system to produce premium-quality fresh wasabi all year round, which rivals the very best-quality wasabi in Japan.

10
MICK THE FORAGER
Mick is a rogue forager who sources anything wild and plentiful. His bounties are often surprises, and he sees beauty and abundance in far-off places.

11
RAMARRO FARM
Oliver Shorthouse and Lisa Joy live and work on their 6 ha (15 acre) farm in Sylvan. They grow unique, often rare and heritage vegetables with care, producing vegetables that make you smile.

12
GREEN EGGS
The 480 ha (1186 acre) Green Eggs farm is located at Great Western near Ararat, in the rolling green foothills of the Grampians. Green Egg farm's eggs are produced ethically with a strong focus on the happiness and welfare of their hens as well as on environmental sustainability.

13
SCHULZ ORGANIC DAIRY
Located in Timboon in South Western Victoria, Schulz Organic Dairy has been at the forefront of organic farming since 1972. Across three generations of dedicated farmers they produce the highest quality milk, yoghurt and cream from their single herd of Friesian and Jersey cows.

14
THE GOOD GRUB
The Good Grub Hub is committed to seeking out the very finest artisanal Japanese ingredients - they are our go to for sourcing Japanese products - from the ubiquitous to the obscure.

15
SOUTHERN CROSS MUSHROOMS
100% Australian Grown and located just outside Melbourne, Southern Cross grows a large range of oyster mushrooms - from blue pearl and king to yellow, pink and black marble - all chemical free. They are fed with natural eucalyptus and soy hull sourced here in Victoria.

AMARANTH SEED is a grain largely produced in Asia and the Americas with a lively, peppery taste. It's available from health food stores and some supermarkets in various forms: flour, seed, flakes, puffed or sprouted.

BONITO FLAKES (katsuobushi) are delicate, shaved flakes of dried and smoked bonito fish, a relative of tuna and mackerel. Katsuobushi has a smoky, savoury flavour and is mainly used as a seasoning in many Japanese dishes including dashi.

CHILLI CRISP SAUCE (Lao Gan Ma brand) is a condiment consisting of slightly crunchy, smoky chilli flakes and a brightly hued red/orange oil. It's often drizzled over dumplings or ramen, adding a warming spicy flavour. It's available in most Asian grocery stores.

CHINESE BLACK VINEGAR (Chinkiang vinegar) is an inky-black, complex vinegar made of glutinous (sticky) rice and malt and aged to produce a rich, mellow, smoky and woody flavour. It's commonly used in Chinese stir-fries, braises and sauces.

CHINESE PRESERVED VEGETABLE (Chinese pickles) is a vegetable fermented by pickling with salt and brine or marinated in soy sauce or savoury bean paste-based mixtures. The vegetables most commonly used are Chinese cabbage (wombok), carrots, cucumbers, winter melon and radishes.

CHRYSANTHEMUM LEAVES also known as crown daisy, have a mildly grassy, herbaceous flavour similar to mustard greens. They can be eaten raw or very briefly steamed, stir-fried or boiled.

DRIED ANCHOVIES are available in many shapes and forms and can be air-dried, sun-dried, smoked or wind-dried. They have an intense umami-packed flavour that's used to enhance soups and stocks. They can also be rehydrated and minced (ground) to add texture to a dish.

DRIED SCALLOPS (conpoy) are cooked scallops that have been sun-dried. They have a strong aroma, a strong, distinctive umami flavour and a vibrant, deep caramel colour. They are usually soaked or steamed prior to being shredded or flaked for use in soups, hotpots, and rice or noodle dishes. They're a key element in XO sauce, providing a rich flavour and texture.

DRIED SHRIMP are regular prawns (shrimp), sun-dried whole to shrink to a fraction of their original size. They're used widely in many Asian cuisines and bring an umami-rich, sweet flavour. Dried shrimp are generally reconstituted and used whole or chopped as a seasoning for many dishes, including soups, salads, sauces, stir-fries and braised dishes. They keep well, refrigerated or frozen.

ESPELETTE PEPPER (Piment D'Espelette) is a Mexican chilli plant. Sun-dried, it has mild heat and a rich, sweet, fruity fragrance reminiscent of tomatoes and roasted capsicum (bell pepper). It adds a sweetness and mild kick to a variety of meat and vegetable dishes and can be purchased as festoons of fresh or dried peppers, ground or puréed or pickled in jars.

FERMENTED CHILLI BEAN PASTE (doubanjiang) is a spicy, salty paste made from fermented broad (fava) beans, soy beans, salt, rice and various spices. Thick and bright red in appearance, it is most often used in Sichuan cuisine, adding spice and depth to braises, stir-fries and rice and noodle dishes.

FERMENTED PLUM EXTRACT (cheong maesil) is made from whole Korean green plums that are fermented with sugar in earthenware vessels for 100 days. The plums break down and liquefy and are then strained to produce a light brown liquid that's sweet, acidic and refreshing. It's used in marinades and sauces, as a tea, a meat tenderiser or in cocktails.

FERMENTED SHRIMP (saeujeot) is a Korean salted and fermented prawn (shrimp) condiment, which is often used in kimchi and dipping pastes. It resembles a pinky beige porridge.

FRIED BREAD (Chinese doughnut or youtiao) consists of long, golden-brown strips of dough that are lightly salted, crunchy on the outside and pillowy soft inside. It's eaten as an accompaniment to both sweet and savoury dishes to absorb flavour and provide contrasting texture.

GINGER VINEGAR is vinegar infused with Japanese pickled ginger, known as gari. It produces a sweet but punchy vinegar traditionally eaten with sushi to clean the palate but it also enhances many fish-based recipes.

GLUTINOUS (STICKY) RICE FLOUR, is a flour made from a variety of glutinous, opaque rice that becomes sticky when cooked. The flour produces a flexible, resilient dough, which can easily take on the flavours of other ingredients and is used in many Chinese bakery products and varieties of dim sum.

GOCHUJANG (Korean chilli paste) is a spicy Korean condiment that is a thick, sticky fermented mixture of chilli, glutinous (sticky) rice flour, soy bean flour, malt flour and seasoning. It has a pungent and savoury flavour, a long shelf life and stores easily in the refrigerator.

GYOZA WRAPPERS are ready-made and rolled dough squares similar to fresh pasta, which can be filled with a meat or vegetable filling and sealed to make dumplings. They're available from Asian supermarkets.

KOMBU POWDER is dried and ground kombu, an edible kelp cultivated in Japan and Korea. Kombu has a salty, smoked, umami-rich dimension used in stocks and soups (notably dashi). It can also be used to season rice when making sushi.

KOREAN CHILLI FLAKES (gochugaru) are bright red with a warm, fruity, capsicum (bell pepper) like flavour and a mild chilli heat. They're made from sun-dried and seeded Korean red chillies and are traditionally used when making kimchi.

KOREAN FISH SAUCE is made from raw anchovies fermented with coarse sea salt, resulting in a pungent, amber-coloured liquid. It's a crucial ingredient in many types of kimchi, both for its taste as well as its fermentation properties.

KOREAN RICE CAKES (tteok) are made from glutinous (sticky) rice flour and water mixed into a paste, which is pounded, rolled into logs and cut into small dumplings or rounds. The rounds can be boiled or fried and have a unique chewy, springy consistency. They're used in both sweet and savoury dishes.

MUSTARD LEAF is the leaf of the mustard plant (Brassica juncea) and is usually emerald green in colour. The leaves have a peppery, slightly bitter flavour and are very versatile. They can be stir-fried, braised and added to soups or stews. Young, tender leaves can be eaten raw in salads.

NORI is seaweed, shredded and rack-dried into sheets in a process similar to paper-making. It's commonly used as a wrap for sushi and onigiri but is also used as a garnish or flavouring in noodle dishes and soups. It is often toasted prior to eating, which enhances its rich, salty umami flavours.

PICKLED MUSTARD greens are used in many Chinese dishes, especially in Sichuan cooking and are available from most Asian grocery stores. They're often used as a side dish, or added to soups, braised dishes and stews. Mustard greens are pickled in an airtight container with sugar, salt and vinegar. They can be preserved for approximately a year.

PICKLED MUSTARD STEM (zha cai) originates from Sichuan, China. It's made from the knobbly, fist-sized green stem of the mustard plant, which is salted, pressed and dried before being rubbed with hot chilli paste and fermented in an earthenware jar. It has a spicy, sour and salty flavour and a uniquely crunchy yet tender texture.

PINK PEPPERCORNS are native to northern Peru. They're mildly spicy and peppery, with a fragrant, sweet/tart flavour.

PORK FLOSS (rousong) is a dried meat product with a light, fluffy texture similar to coarse cotton. It's made by stewing cuts of pork in a sweetened soy sauce mixture until the muscle fibres can be teased apart. This teased meat is then oven-dried, and then dry-fried in a wok. It's often used as a topping for dishes like congee and as a filling for buns and pastries and has a salty, meaty flavour like jerky.

POTATO STARCH, or potato flour, is extracted from potatoes by crushing them to release starch grains. This starch is then washed and dried to a powder. It's used as a thickener in baking and as a water binder or gluing agent.

PRESERVED SNOW VEGETABLE (potherb mustard) is a green leafy vegetable with a tender stalk, which is eaten as a side dish and also added to stir-fries and braises. The raw vegetable is finely shredded, salted and kneaded before being strained and kept in an airtight container. The process softens the snow vegetable and gives it an aromatic, slightly fermented flavour.

PUFFED WILD RICE is created by heating a small amount of oil in a large pot, and adding wild rice that has been boiled, drained and oven-dried. The pot is then covered with a lid to allow the rice to pop, similar to the process of making popcorn. Puffed rice is often used as a garnish, and adds additional texture and an earthy flavour.

RICE WINE VINEGAR is made by fermenting the sugars from rice into an alcohol such as wine, then further fermenting the wine into acetic acid. Rice wine vinegar is mild and slightly sweet and works well in salad dressings and dipping sauces. There are many varieties made from different kinds of rice: brown, black glutinous, red yeast etc., which all offer different flavour profiles.

ROASTED SHRIMP PASTE is made from prawns (shrimp), mashed, mixed with salt and fermented over a period of weeks, which results in a paste ranging in colour from light to dark brown and in texture from soft to rock hard. Big and bold with a salty, fishy flavour it's used in everything from curries and stir-fries to sauces and relishes and can be used (sparingly) like a seasoning. It's best to roast shrimp paste before using in cooking, by wrapping the paste in foil and placing it under the grill (broiler) for 10 minutes, or by pan-frying it in a small amount of oil. Once roasted, the paste can be pounded into a powder.

ROCK SUGAR is refined crystallised sugar that is opaque and gold-coloured, and comes in irregularly shaped lumps of varying sizes, which require breaking up before use. It has a clear taste, with no caramel tones and is not as sweet as regular white granulated sugar.

ROLLED RICE NOODLES (banh cuon) are made from a thin, wide sheet of steamed rice batter that's then rolled and filled. The rice sheet is extremely thin and delicate, and is traditionally made by steaming the slightly fermented rice batter on a cloth that's stretched over a pot of boiling water. At home, they can be made in a non-stick frying pan.

SCHOOL PRAWNS (shrimp) are usually eaten whole with their shell on, and are typical in many Asian cuisines. They have a distinct taste, sweeter than most other prawns and are typically eaten fried.

SHAOXING RICE WINE is made from fermented, brown glutinous (sticky) rice and is used both as a beverage and in cooking. Amber-coloured, aromatic and pleasantly nutty tasting, it can be mixed into dumpling fillings, added to marinades for roasted meats such as char siu pork, combined with seasonings for stir-fries, or simmered with soy sauce and sugar for red-cooked dishes.

SHICHIMI TOGARASHI (Japanese chilli powder) is a common Japanese spice mixture containing seven ingredients. A typical blend may contain coarsely ground red chilli pepper, ground sansho, roasted orange peel, black sesame seed, white sesame seed, hemp seed, ground ginger and nori.

SHISO is a herb belonging to the mint family with large teardrop-shaped leaves with serrated edges. Its distinctive, almost perfumed flavour has hints of basil, mint and citrus. Shiso complements many dishes, from meat and seafood to vegetables and is often used as an accompaniment to sushi and sashimi.

SICHUAN PEPPERCORN (Chinese coriander) is a common spice in Chinese cuisine. The finely ground powder is one of the ingredients for five-spice powder. Sichuan pepper's unique aroma and flavour is not hot or pungent like black, white or chilli peppers but instead has a slight lemony overtone and creates a tingly numbness in the mouth.

SRIRACHA SAUCE is a bright red, multi-purpose hot sauce made from red chilli peppers, garlic, vinegar, salt and sugar. It is hot and tangy with just a hint of sweetness, and is often served as a condiment in Thai, Vietnamese and Chinese cooking. Once a secret of Asian kitchens and restaurants, it is now available in supermarkets.

13-SPICE is a Chinese spice powder consisting of 13 Chinese herbals: zikou, amomum fruit, nutmeg, cinnamon, clove, pepper, aniseed, fennel, costustoot, angelica root, sand ginger, galangal and dried ginger.

TORORO KOMBU consists of thin, long sheets or flakes of dried kombu (kelp). It is softened in a vinegar marinade before being shaved and added to a variety of soup, rice and noodle dishes.

UNI is the Japanese name for the edible part of the sea urchin. It ranges in colour from rich gold to light yellow with a creamy consistency. Uni has a light, sweet, somewhat briny flavour.

WAKAME is sea vegetable that grows on rocks around the coast of Japan. Wakame is sun-dried to retain its nutritional value and flavour. It has a subtly sweet flavour and is most often served in salads and soups such as miso.

WHITE SOY SAUCE (shoyu) is clearer and thinner than traditional Chinese dark soy sauce. It has a light amber colour and infuses foods without darkening them. Shoyu uses an even ratio of soy beans and wheat, resulting in a sweeter, milder flavour that often accompanies sushi and sashimi, seafood, clear soups, tofu and steamed vegetables.

YUZU JUICE Yuzu is a citrus fruit from East Asia that resembles a small grapefruit. It is yellow or green with an even skin and tart flavour, similar to grapefruit, with hints of mandarin. It is rarely eaten as a whole fruit — the juice and zest are used in Japanese cuisine as a seasoning, similar to the way lemon is used in other cuisines.

YUZU KOSHO is a type of Japanese seasoning, a condiment paste made from a mix of chilli peppers, yuzu peel and salt, which is allowed to ferment. It is intensely fragrant, hot and zesty and enhances many dishes such as hotpots, soups and sashimi.

ACKNOWLEDGEMENTS

It takes many people to open and run a restaurant and, in some ways, just as many to bring a cookbook to life. I have many people to thank for their contribution to this book.

Michaela Webb was the driving force behind this book's unique and beautiful design. Michaela's approach to design and her enthusiasm for the medium in which she works is inspirational. Thanks also to the entire team at Round especially Robert Nudds, Florence Li and Bianca Lazzaro for their attention to detail and professionalism.

Michael Harden for his wonderful words, sage advice and good taste. It was a pleasure to work with someone with such a clear understanding and appreciation of the restaurant world and what we do.

Earl Carter is one of Australia's most respected photographers, not just because his photographs are beautiful to look at, but because they also provoke emotion. It was a privilege to work with Earl on this book. He has an innate understanding of what I do and manages to find beauty in both the refined and the everyday.

There are many people who have contributed to the success of Supernormal, now and over the past few years. To all the staff I have had the privilege of working with, thank you. John Paul Twomey, Ben Pigott, Rebecca Lang and Archan Chan: your commitment and skill is inspiring to me and everyone else who is lucky enough to work with you.

Our busy restaurant is held together and run with professional calm by a dedicated team of front-of-house professionals who care. Oliver Shorthouse, Chris Handel and Leanne Altmann, thank you.

Our first head chef at Golden Fields, Arnie Josue, and Todd Moses have contributed greatly and both influenced where Supernormal is today.

Thank you to Polly Gollings for her kitchen prowess, once again.

Thanks to Clare Forster for your continued guidance. Thanks also to Jane Willson and Ariana Klepac at Hardie Grant, for your editorial support and confidence.

Projects of Imagination designed the interior and branding for Supernormal. The beauty in Supernormal is testament to Dion Hall's vision and considered sensibility. Co-founder and director of Projects of imagination, Nick Cox, created our unique and original brand experience. Thank you Nick for your thoughtful, playful and timeless design.

To Lou Weis and Broached Commissions, thank you for your support and friendship and for the introduction to the beautiful work of Azuma Makoto and his Paludarium.

Anna Vu #goodfoodcrapdrawing, thank you for agreeing to contribute — we love your work.

I am lucky to work in a thriving dining scene like the one we have in Melbourne. A special thank you to all our customers for their support and good will.

Thank you to my family, Jo, Pia, Tove, Luca and Henry, for their continued support and for all the joy they bring.

Importantly I would like to acknowledge and thank all of my staff, both past and present. Without you, none of this would be possible.

Thank you.

THIS EDITION PUBLISHED IN 2023
BY HARDIE GRANT BOOKS,
AN IMPRINT OF
HARDIE GRANT PUBLISHING
FIRST PUBLISHED IN 2015

HARDIE GRANT BOOKS (MELBOURNE)
Wurundjeri Country
Building 1, 658 Church Street
Richmond, Victoria 3121
hardiegrant.com/au/books

HARDIE GRANT BOOKS (UK)
5th & 6th Floors
52–54 Southwark Street
London SE1 1UN
hardiegrant.com/uk/books

Supernormal
ISBN 978 176145 001 3

 A catalogue record for this
book is available from the
National Library of Australia

Hardie Grant acknowledges the Traditional
Owners of the country on which we work,
the Wurundjeri people of the Kulin nation and
the Gadigal people of the Eora nation, and
recognises their continuing connection to the
land, waters and culture. We pay our respects
to their Elders past and present

Printed in China by
Leo Paper Products LTD

Colour reproduction by
Splitting Image Colour Studio

The paper this book is printed on is from
FSC®-certified forests and other sources.
FSC® promotes environmentally responsible,
socially beneficial and economically viable
management of the world's forests.

PUBLISHER
MICHAEL HARRY

EDITOR
MICHAEL HARDEN

COPY EDITOR
ARIANA KLEPAC

COVER DESIGNER
DANIEL NEW

INTERNAL DESIGNER
STUDIO ROUND

PHOTOGRAPHER
EARL CARTER

PRODUCTION MANAGER
TODD RECHNER

PRODUCTION COORDINATOR
JESSICA HARVIE